THIS ART

THIS ART

poems about poetry

edited by Michael Wiegers

A COPPER CANYON PRESS ANTHOLOGY

Printed in the United States of America.

Cover art: *Rocky Pier,* Tsuda, Shikoku, Japan, 2001, toned gelatin silver print by Michael Kenna. Courtesy of the artist and G. Gibson Gallery.

Copper Canyon Press is in residence under the auspices of the Centrum Foundation at Fort Worden State Park in Port Townsend, Washington. Centrum sponsors artist residencies, education workshops for Washington State students and teachers, Blues, Jazz, and Fiddle Tunes festivals, classical music performances, and the Port Townsend Writers' Conference.

LIBRARY OF CONGRESS CATALOGING-IN-PUBLICATION DATA
This art: poems about poetry / edited by Michael Wiegers.
p.cm.-- (A Copper Canyon Press Anthology)
ISBN 1-55659-184-5 (alk. paper)
1. Poetry--Authorship--Poetry. 2. Poetics--Poetry. 3. American poetry. I. Wiegers, Michael. II. Series.
PS595.P63T47 2003
811.008'0357--dc21
2003001052

98765432

COPPER CANYON PRESS
Post Office Box 271
Port Townsend, Washington 98368
www.coppercanyonpress.org

CONTENTS

In the beginner's mind there are many possibilities,
but in the expert's there are few.

SHUNRYU SUZUKI ROSHI

When cutting an axe handle with an axe,
surely the model is at hand.

LU CHI

INTRODUCTION

Anthologizing poets around a common subject in order to explore its meaning is often a woefully well-intentioned disservice to poetry. The art of poetry thrives on unpredictability and rebellion. It is the nature of poets to disagree and even to be disagreeable. Nowhere is this truer than when a poem's subject is poetry itself. History is filled with poets arguing over their art: What is good poetry? Bad poetry? What *is* poetry? Theories have been forwarded, arguments made, sides taken, schools created. Poets are compelled by tradition to defend their art, but they write from a contemporary setting and are confronted by an art that is made up, in part, by common, everyday *words.* So what makes poetry *art?* How is it different from prose arts? Why does it matter so much to those who love it? Often the loudest arguments on behalf of poetry, the answers and theories of what poetry is, how it is different, and whether it matters, are made in prose. Meanwhile, the more convincing arguments are made in poems.

As one of the oldest art forms, poetry carries a large cultural weight on its back, a reciprocal body of information and associations that inform and support the form. Poets often work out of acknowledged traditions and lineages, and their poems may be filled with allusions and secondary references. It is easy to be intimidated by poetry because of so much background information. But this information, while rewarding and of interest to the poetry reader, is not always necessary in order to enjoy a poem.

Present-day mythology suggests that few people read or care about poetry. Accordingly, most book readers have supposedly been frightened away from the art. But in a country that values the marketplace, even lowly poetry can have its industry. I'd argue that there are more poetry readers than ever before. Publishers produce over 1,000 poetry books each year. Most universities now have M.F.A. programs in poetry writing. Critics, arguing for their share of the market, view these developments positively or negatively. Fortunately, poetry outlasts the arguments. In the words of the eighteenth century Vietnamese poet Hồ Xuân Hương, "Only poetry lasts."

One reason it lasts is because there is no single way to read a poem. A poem is irreducible. It is okay to *not* understand everything a poem offers upon first reading. Occasionally some poets even learn from their readers another way to read their own poems. One need not be an expert, but one should enter a poem with humility. James Galvin writes, "Let us begin with a simple line." We start with a line, pay attention, and the rest follows: "The line draws us in, / Requiring further lines, / Engendering curves, verticals, diagonals, / Urging shades, shapes, figures." As we start the process of poetry—reading or writing it—we never know where it might lead. It's a process of discovery, a process of opening oneself to not-knowing. It has always been this way. Poems taught the preliterate how to live. Poems have passed along history's great narratives and religious beliefs. Poetry helps us pay closer attention to the world around us. We write poetry for the sake of poetry, and we read it, similarly, for the sake of what is found there. Poetry is as natural as breathing, not a cause for intimidation.

Kenneth Rexroth wrote, "The centuries have changed little in this art, / The subjects are still the same." But the poets have changed, and just as there are many ways of reading poetry, there are even more reasons for writing it. One of the subjects that has remained the same throughout the centuries is the subject of poetry itself. A poem about poetry is a paradox (and thus fitting for the poet's proclivity for disagreement). No matter how independent a poet may seem, in writing a poem about poetry he or she joins a long literary tradition which demands that the poet break from tradition, that he or she not be restricted by art, but be liberated by it. Hayden Carruth writes, "A poem is not an expression, nor is it an object. Yet it somewhat partakes of both. What a poem is / Is never to be known, for which I have learned to be grateful." In asking what makes a poem succeed, poets ask also why they write. They question humanity's place in the world and art's role in that world, specifically the art of lyrics and narratives.

To write about poetry is to believe that there are answers to some of the questions poets ask of their art, or at least that there are reasons for writing it. A poem about the art of poetry is not born out of a lack of subject matter but, rather, arises out of an excess that transcends the humanly possible; it arises out of the questions one cannot answer. How can the poet make sense of the world, and why should he even try? How does one order chaos or seek the appropriate forms for expression? To where does the poem lead? Why does anyone make art? Who will read this poem? The answers lead invariably to more questions. This process of entering a poem leads both the giver of the gift and its recipient toward a critical engagement with the poem, and through that to a larger engagement with the world. The poet brings life to writing a poem; the reader brings life to reading it. Through this process the *ars poetica,* the poem about poetry, has helped sustain the very art it addresses.

Copper Canyon Press started with this intimate dedication to poetry-for-its-own-sake because poetry changes lives. Over thirty years ago, Founding Editor Sam Hamill recognized that he had been deeply affected by poetry and wanted to return the gift that poetry had given him. Together with Tree Swenson and William O'Daly he started his publishing legacy first by printing poems on a letterpress, one poem at a time, the type set and printed by hand. Poem followed poem as slowly books were built. Many books—and a handful of volunteers and staff members—followed over the years, but the individual poem always remained central to Copper Canyon Press. Each book started simply, first with a line of type, then a page, then a book, with Hamill repeating a one-on-one relationship, as editor, as printer, as type-setter, as translator, as poet, and most of all as reader. He has accumulated a broad knowledge of poetry, receiving the very gift he gave away.

Rebecca Seiferle writes, "We all stumble into ourselves / like this, fitting our fingers to the shape of letters, / while the page gallops out of our reach." I have heard Hamill say similar words and have read them in his books. In another poem, John Balaban asks what Hamill must occasionally have wondered when he was just starting out, "Will the ancient tales still tell us new truths? /

Will the myriad world surrender new metaphor?" Adding to the conversation, David Budbill echoes the Japanese poet Issa, "since we will always have a suffering world, / we must also always have a song." As Hamill and Copper Canyon Press reciprocated the gift of poetry, the gift to others grew. And by increments—one poem at a time—lives were changed, lives enriched. Each poem marks a beginning.

Most readers can remember their beginnings in poetry. In 1988 I was working as a bookseller when I received a little box of catalogs from Copper Canyon Press's new distributor. One of the few offerings was a new *Selected Poems* by Thomas McGrath. I hadn't read him and didn't know anything about the Press. But here was a publishing house that clearly was not afraid of poetry, a publisher that was devoted to it. I ordered McGrath's book. *You can start the poetry now,* a voice commands in one poem. And I did. I was a beginner entering a new world of poetry (a world sometimes seemingly at odds with the rest of the world). It was one poem, by one poet, read by one reader.

A few years later I returned to Copper Canyon Press via Hayden Carruth's *Collected Shorter Poems,* a book that gathered forty-five years of his work, through 1991. I had never read Carruth before, either; most of his books had been out of print. I soon wondered how it could be that he wasn't better known. Again a single poem quickly caught my attention, "The Impossible Indispensability of the Ars Poetica". Midway through it, Carruth asks, "Why otherwise is the earliest always the most important, the formative? The Iliad, the Odyssey, the Book of Genesis, / These were acts of love, I mean deeply felt gestures, which continuously bestow upon us / What we are." My world started expanding. This poem taught me (and continues to teach me) a great deal about poetry. Carruth's poems changed my life, though I didn't know then that they would. His poems led me to other discoveries, including other books and poets published by Copper Canyon Press.

Since that first reading of "The Impossible Indispensability of the Ars Poetica" I've found that I keep returning to it as one might to a prayer. Some pray for guidance in their lives; I may not be a religious man, but I have poems. (Even as I write this I hear Carruth's words, from another poem in this anthology, echoing in my ears.) I believe there is a sort of continuation given to our lives via the writing and reading of poetry. Whenever I question what it is we do here at Copper Canyon Press, whenever I hear the din of critics theorizing about the relevance of poetry or I hear a reviewer apologize for not being able to review poetry, I can usually find solace (answers, too!) in a poem. I have often returned to Carruth's book. Why poetry? *The poem is a gift, a bestowal.*

When I began assembling this anthology I expected to battle an overabundance of the first-person pronoun. Instead, I was surprised to find that the second-person "you" abounds. This lesson was always right there in the "Impossible Indispensability of the Ars Poetica," but it took reading many other poems for me to understand that Carruth's "you" was inclusive. It was me, too. It is *you,* the reader of the poem, you who hold this book. The poet is asking you to engage in a very intimate exchange. Poets expose themselves to a peculiar sort of vulnerability; through this vulnerability, this giving away, the poet literally gives life to words, and gives the life of the world around us—to readers, to complete strangers, to those willing to accept their gift: the labor of words turned into artful expression. The gift of the poem is a doorway which leads us out of ourselves and to others.

Consider some of history's tragic figures: Miklós Radnóti on his death march, or Nazim Hikmet in a Turkish prison, or Ovid on his island. The list goes on. Even in the most extreme cases of isolation, poetry connects each of us to the world beyond the individual self. It embraces a process that goes back to the beginning of the spoken word. Nothing, not even the creative act, is self-originating. We write—and publish—in a language given to us through the centuries. No literary form addresses this more directly than the poem about poetry, the poem that, as Carruth asserts, "gives it all to you." Contrary to the conventional belief that poetry is an exclusive art, poetry is an art infinitely inviting and infinitely inclusive.

The eclecticism of tastes represented in this anthology—each exploring the same common subject—is not an isolation of an artistic sensibility, but a liberation. The Copper Canyon Press aesthetic arises out of the determined independence that sustained the original founding of the Press. A great poem can't be reduced. When I consider the poetry of David Lee alongside that of Hồ Xuân Hương, or Su Tung-p'o alongside Antonio Porchia, or Erin Belieu alongside Olga Broumas, I find a few similarities that might be ascribed to a house aesthetic, and I enjoy those similarities immensely. But a greater joy obtains from the *differences* found in these poems. Each poet has his or her own way of viewing poetry, and through it, the world. The capacity to incorporate these differences—while still maintaining a devotion to the art of poetry—has marked the books published by Copper Canyon Press throughout its history and, with a small amount of luck, will be a signature of the books we've yet to publish. *You can start the poetry now.*

MICHAEL WIEGERS

THIS ART

ART CLASS

Let us begin with a simple line,
Drawn as a child would draw it,
To indicate the horizon,

More real than the real horizon,
Which is less than line,
Which is visible abstraction, a ratio.

The line ravishes the page with implications
Of white earth, white sky!

The horizon moves as we move,
Making us feel central.
But the horizon is an empty shell—

Strange radius whose center is peripheral.
As the horizon draws us on, withdrawing,
The line draws us in,

Requiring further lines,
Engendering curves, verticals, diagonals,
Urging shades, shapes, figures…

What should we place, in all good faith,
On the horizon? A stone?
An empty chair? A submarine?

Take your time. Take it easy.
The horizon will not stop abstracting us.

JAMES GALVIN

"ONCE I GOT A POSTCARD"

Once I got a postcard from the Fiji Islands
with a picture of sugarcane harvest. Then I realized
that nothing at all is exotic in itself.
There is no difference between digging potatoes
in our Mutiku garden
and sugarcane harvesting in Viti Levu.
Everything that is is very ordinary
or, rather, neither ordinary nor strange.
Far-off lands and foreign peoples are a dream,
a dreaming with open eyes
somebody does not wake from.
It's the same with poetry—seen from afar
it's something special, mysterious, festive.
No, poetry is even less
special than a sugarcane plantation or potato field.
Poetry is like sawdust coming from under the saw
or soft yellowish shavings from a plane.
Poetry is washing hands in the evening
or a clean handkerchief that my late aunt
never forgot to put in my pocket.

JAAN KAPLINSKI
Translated from the Estonian
by Jaan Kaplinski,
Riina Tamm, and
Sam Hamill

ALWAYS ON THE TRAIN

Writing poems about writing poems
is like rolling bales of hay in Texas.
Nothing but the horizon to stop you.

But consider the railroad's edge of metal trash;
bird perches, miles of telephone wires.
What is so innocent as grazing cattle?
If you think about it, it turns into words.

Trash is so cheerful, flying up
like grasshoppers in front of the reaper.
The dust devil whirls it aloft: bronze candy wrappers,
squares of clear plastic—windows on a house of air.

Below the weedy edge in last year's mat,
red and silver beer cans.
In bits blown equally everywhere,
the gaiety of flying paper
and the black high flung patterns of flocking birds.

RUTH STONE

ON THE SUBJECT OF POETRY

I do not understand the world, Father.
By the millpond at the end of the garden
There is a man who slouches listening
To the wheel revolving in the stream, only
There is no wheel there to revolve.

He sits in the end of March, but he sits also
In the end of the garden; his hands are in
His pockets. It is not expectation
On which he is intent, nor yesterday
To which he listens. It is a wheel turning.

When I speak, Father, it is the world
That I must mention. He does not move
His feet nor so much as raise his head
For fear he should disturb the sound he hears
Like a pain without a cry, where he listens.

I do not think I am fond, Father,
Of the way in which always before he listens
He prepares himself by listening. It is
Unequal, Father, like the reason
For which the wheel turns, though there is no wheel.

I speak of him, Father, because he is
There with his hands in his pockets, in the end
Of the garden listening to the turning
Wheel that is not there, but it is the world,
Father, that I do not understand.

W.S. MERWIN

GEO-BESTIARY #X

I know a private mountain range with a big bowl in its center that you find by following the narrowest creek bed, sometimes crawling until you struggle through a thicket until you reach two large cupped hands of stone in the middle of which is a hill, a promontory, which would be called a mountain back home. There is iron in this hill and it sucks down summer lightning, thousands and thousands of strokes through time, shattering the gigantic top into a field of undramatic crystals that would bring a buck a piece at a rock show. I was here in a dark time and stood there and said, "I have put my poem in order on the threshold of my tongue," quoting someone from long, long ago, then got the hell off the mountain due to tremors of undetermined source. Later that night sleeping under an oak a swarm of elf owls (*Micrathene whitneyi*) descended to a half-dozen feet above my head and a thousand white sycamores undulated in the full moon, obviously the living souls of lightning strokes upside down along the arroyo bed. A modern man, I do not make undue connections though my heart wrenches daily against the unknowable, almighty throb and heave of the universe against my skin that sings a song for which we haven't quite found the words.

JIM HARRISON

THE ALLURE OF FORMS

Blissful dance. Scream
of the shadows in light.
Night that pours its animal shrill
into the morning's joy.
There it ramifies,
bursts, intertwines itself. It blossoms
on its clearest edge. It's the allure of forms
in their steep nearness, their engulfed
proximity. Rivers become entangled with, yet do not merge,
an obscure lightning, an arborescent
flame. Fauna
sliding between the blazes.
It's the pleasure of opposites: the scattered pondering,
the swarming and resonant jungle.

CORAL BRACHO
translated from the Spanish
by Mónica de la Torre

365 POEMS

They will be floating from my mouth like doves
like bright scarves from the sleeves of the magician.
Look, I am spinning five of them over my head.
It has been a bad dream when I
forgot to twirl one like a flag every day,
to walk into town like a parade
with flutes and drums, with timbrels.
They will be chariots drawn by lions.
They will be gazelles and leopards.
They will fly around me like a flock of birds.
They will be my traveling companions.
They will gnaw at me day and night
like minnows, or devour me whole like the whale.
I will stand among them as among trees of a forest,
calling, these are all mine!
They will tell me secrets.
Wherever I go like the roll of drums,
salvos of guns, rockets kindling the air,
they will arrive day and night.
I will beg them to go away.
They will torment me like gnats,
swoop by like hawks at noon, bewilder my dreams at evening.
They will say, welcome home.

ANN STANFORD

POETRY

Invited onto the grounds of the god,
who decides what words mean,
we are amazed at the world
perfect at last. Gold fish, gold finches, gold watches,
trash blasted into crystal, all
twilights supporting one final sunset
with slender fingers of consolation.
A little reality goes a long way,
far off in the distance the weak sea
beaches its blue whales, the small sky
melds the stars into one
serious fire, burning eternally
out of control, our earth.
But here we are visiting
the plutonium factory dazzling
to the eye, the one good one remaining
to us in our wisdom. We have concluded
that automatic, volcanic sunrises and sunsets
where light trips on the same cardboard vine
are blinding, and we would rather fail
painfully slowly than survive a copy
of the world perfect at last. Yet we are
impressed by the real thing, which we walk
like dew upon flesh, suddenly lubricated and translucent
beyond our dreamiest desires, hard-pressed
to object. Consoled that there is so little
difference between the terrible and the real,
we admire the powerful appleseeds bobbing
in the dewy pools, we cannot help
but enjoy their greeny spring, and it is only by resting
on the miraculous grass, wildly uniform, mildly serene,

that we sense
with our secret selves, the little bit we left behind and remember, that we are out of our element, that we are being made into words even as we speak.

JANE MILLER

VOICES
(an excerpt)

When you seem to be listening to my words, they seem to be your words, with me listening.

*

What words say does not last. The words last. Because words are always the same, and what they say is never the same.

*

My "I" has gone farther and farther away from me. Today it is my farthest "you."

*

When you and the truth speak to me I do not listen to the truth. I listen to you.

*

Situated in some nebulous distance I do what I do so that the universal balance of which I am a part may remain a balance.

*

He who has made a thousand things and he who has made none, both feel the same desire: to make something.

*

Man talks about everything, and he talks about everything as though the understanding of everything were all inside him.

*

One lives in the hope of becoming a memory.

*

Nothing that is complete breathes.

*

He who tells the truth says almost nothing.

*

When I come upon some idea that is not of this world, I feel as though this world had grown wider.

*

Would there be this eternal seeking if the found existed?

*

We tear life out of life to use it for looking at itself.

*

All truth acts out from the newborn. From that which was not.

*

All things pronounce names.

*

This world understands nothing but words, and you have come into it with almost none.

ANTONIO PORCHIA
translated from the Spanish
by W.S. Merwin

WHAT WE NEED WORDS FOR

Each morning, his baby fingers clack
on the electronic keys of the obsolete typewriter
that my father left us when he died,
and what my son hears and loves is the sound
of his own fingers clattering into the world, the zing
of the carriage return, the space bar like a runaway train
clicking through the letters that he is only beginning
to recognize, the hunt and peck
of his own name.

We all stumble into ourselves
like this, fitting our fingers to the shape of letters,
while the page gallops out of our reach,
and, though he's only five, it's loss that drives him
to the words, trying to pick out his own name
among whatever is attached to himself, whatever
he longs to answer, relating each day
a letter to his sister, now gone from home,
far away in college.

The page, when it rolls off the cylinder,
is full of the rhythm of his furious
digits, all drive and urgency of expression,
a jumble of letters and numbers, not words,
not legible text, but a sea of drift,
and, yet, at times, in the broken lines,
a name, a word, floats up into view—
the first legibility of the heart, its exacting
infancy—*lluv luve yur broder Jacob.*

REBECCA SEIFERLE

GEORGI BORISOV IN PARIS

The Slavic poet sips his morning vodka, his mind
as troubled as the river sliding down below
the twenty-second floor of his apartment on the Seine
where a barge cuts the surface to thread Pont Mirabeau.

He knows that words are fading from books.
From poems of Pushkin, from Apollonaire's,
from poems he wrote when talking in his dreams.
Words are disappearing, leaving pages bare.

Next door, an office complex bustles like a hive,
its workers tending cells inside the glassed-in combs.
He stares into their cubicles. It sours his vodka.
Their tower has become... a heap of drying bones.

But what can poets do about the missing words, gone
even from those lips that longed to say them—like wishes
floating off above the river, like coins
tossed from barges, bridges, *bateaux-mouches?*

Where else is this happening? Is it happening at home?
In a world reduced to billboards, he would be totally unnerved.
The strangely exiled poet has been drinking for ten days
but this has only sharpened his worry about the words...

JOHN BALABAN

SPEECH ALONE

It happens that one pronounces
a few words just for oneself
alone on this strange earth
then the small white flower
the pebble like all those that went before
the sprig of stubble
find themselves reunited
at the foot of the gate
which one opens slowly
to enter the house of clay
while chairs, table, cupboard,
blaze in a sun of glory.

JEAN FOLLAIN
translated from the French
by W.S. Merwin

ARS POETICA

They wanted from us
loud despairs, ear-
splitting syntactical tricks, our guts
hung up to the light, privacy
dusted off and displayed, in ways
elliptical and clever, or
in a froth of spleen—details
of the damages, musings on divorce,
ashtrays from motels: films shot
on location, life made almost real
by its private dislocations. This
they said, was the true
grit, the way it is, no lies, the heart
laid open as a pancake griddle to the awful
heat of rage, rage and desire, coiled beneath
and glowing, until even a drop of sweat
or ink, let fall in its vicinity,
would sizzle. And over all, the big I
swollen like a jellyfish, quivering
and venomous. These things were
our imperative: the poet
in his stained T-shirt, all gripes
and belly, and, well, so *personable*—
my god, so like ourselves!
Oh yes, the women poets too, so
unashamed, ripping off their masks
like nylon stockings.

***

And all the time, the shy and shapely
mind, like some Eurydice, wanders—
darkened by veils, a shade
with measured footsteps. So many things are gone
and the end of the world looms
like a shark's fin on the flats of our horizon.
Fatigue sets in, and the wind rises.
The door is swinging on its hinges—the room
pried open, the one upstairs in Bluebeard's castle.
They have been hanging there a long time
in their bridal dresses, from hooks,
by their own long hair.
The wind that makes them sway until
they seem almost alive
is like the rush of our compassion.
Yes, now we remember them all
and the sea with its unchanging heaving—a grief
as deep and as dactylic as the voice of Homer,
and, as we turn another way, we lay the past out
on Achilles' shield, abandon it to earth,
our common ground—the bridal hope, its murder,
the old, old story, perpetual
as caring: the scant human store
that is so strangely self-restoring
and whose sufficiency
is our continual surprise.

ELEANOR WILNER

THOUGHTS ON A NIGHT JOURNEY

A slight wind stirs grasses along the bank.
A lone boat sails with a mast in the night.
The stars are pulled down to the vast plain,
and the moon bobs in the river's flow.

My name will never be famous in literature:
I have resigned office from sickness and age.
Drifting and drifting, what am I
but a solitary gull between earth and heaven?

Tu Fu
translated from the Chinese
by Arthur Sze

THE PURCHASE

Once you've bought into the suspension of disbelief
the tour guide lays suspense on you. And
while you are in that state, he pours all the details—all
the things you are not necessarily interested in—over
you like a rinse after a soaping: all
places named after the abalone in California,
Geodetic Survey reports,
a map of the first route to the Pacific Coast,
a treatise on whaling,
a history of San Mateo.
And before you realize you are irritated
by the delay, you feel pleased to learn
something new and useful.
And so what if it was a trick?
Sometimes it is necessary
to buy a thing you don't want.

CLARENCE MAJOR

YOU CAN START THE POETRY NOW, OR: NEWS FROM CRAZY HORSE

—I guess all I'm trying to say is I saw Crazy Horse die for
a split level swimming pool in a tree-house owned by
a Pawnee–Warner Brothers psychiatrist about three
hundred feet above —

You can start the poetry now.

—above City Hall kind of sacred ground where they shot the Great
Buddha wild drags in the atomic parking lot but no good
gas seems I remember —

You can Start the Poetry now.

—remember John Grass, University of North Dakota '69, did not
complete his thesis sort of half-classed Indian was too busy
fighting Custer to write he wrote last of the ten
million Mohicanos when the physicists began changing red-
skins to greenbacks it wasn't—

YOU can Start the Poetry NOW!

—wasn't Gall who built all those slaveways after lifting the weight
of the guilt hair Custer's wasn't it Gall or Crazy
Horse Sitting Bull or Rain-In-The-Face wigged him it was
later they died on the tailfins it makes you want to shoot horse-
power capitalists who done it —

YOU CAN START the POETRY now!!

—who done it it's between the gilt heir and the surplus value
grand cost of counting coup in the swimming pools stolen from
the Teton Sioux first ones I ever saw with built-in jails it's
capitalism unlimited the american Platonic year what I
can't get straight is the white antelope they're using for
money it's the —

START THE POETRY! START THE POETRY NOW!!

—it's the quarters and halves or maybe the whole antelope Buck that
gets me it's the cutting up of the Buffalo Bread it's all *them*
goddam swimming pools full of shot horses it's Christ Indians
and revolutionaries charging full-tilt at the psychiatrists'
couches and being blasted with the murderous electrical hot
missionary money of hell-by-installments it's all of us pining
and starving surrounded by the absolute heavenly pemmican-
charisma that Geronimo invented it's the—

*START THE POETRY!! GOD*DAMN *IT!!*
START THE POETRY!! START THE POETRY NOW!!

THOMAS MCGRATH

THE USEFUL

In the colors of the useful
that of gray and black material
of steel blue
of rusty flecks
some take shelter in order to live.

Sometimes one hears their words
their appeals to the rain
to the sun, to the green leaves

and the things around them unite
to be reflected in their eyes.

JEAN FOLLAIN
translated from the French
by W.S. Merwin

LOVE POEM

...Do not write love poems;
avoid at first those forms
that are too facile and common-
place: they are the most difficult...

R. M. Rilke in *Letters to a Young Poet*

There are too many similes for bed—
nothing at all like the things I've said
scribbling late this last hour;

not like the boats I've rigged, or rivers either,
designed for us to float. Metaphor
sinks what I meant to say.

And about what Rilke says, I know even
his angels won't save me now; heaven
is much too terrible to leave.

So all you get to know is that I'm trying,
my tongue *not* a stupid girl crying
down my throat, wet and speechless.

ERIN BELIEU

THESE POEMS, SHE SAID

These poems, these poems,
these poems, she said, are poems
with no love in them. These are the poems of a man
who would leave his wife and child because
they made noise in his study. These are the poems
of a man who would murder his mother to claim
the inheritance. These are the poems of a man
like Plato, she said, meaning something I did not
comprehend but which nevertheless
offended me. These are the poems of a man
who would rather sleep with himself than with women,
she said. These are the poems of a man
with eyes like a drawknife, with hands like a pickpocket's
hands, woven of water and logic
and hunger, with no strand of love in them. These
poems are as heartless as birdsong, as unmeant
as elm leaves, which if they love love only
the wide blue sky and the air and the idea
of elm leaves. Self-love is an ending, she said,
and not a beginning. Love means love
of the thing sung, not of the song or the singing.
These poems, she said...
                                        You are, he said,
beautiful.
          That is not love, she said rightly.

ROBERT BRINGHURST

POETICS

The boy is aware that the tree is alive.
If the tender leaves force themselves open,
bursting ruthlessly into the light, the hard bark
must suffer extremely. And it lives in silence.
The whole world is covered with plants that suffer
in light, not daring even to breathe.
A tender light, its source unknown to the boy.
It's evening already, but each trunk stands out
against a magical background. In a moment it's dark.

The boy—and some men remain boys
for too long—who once was afraid of the dark,
walks down the street, not minding the twilight
that darkens the houses. He listens, head bowed,
to a distant memory. In the emptied-out streets
that seem like piazzas, a grave silence gathers.
A person can feel he's alone in a forest
where the trees are enormous. The light
shudders through streetlamps. The houses
are dazzling, transparent in the bluish vapor,
and the boy raises his eyes. The distant silence
that can tighten a person's breath has flowered
in the sudden light. These are the boy's
ancient trees. And the light is the spell of that time.

And somebody now is walking silently past,
through the diaphanous circle. On the street, no one
ever reveals the pain that gnaws at their life.
They move quickly, as if absorbed in their stride,

their great shadows staggering. Their faces are furrowed,
their eyes full of grief, but no one complains.
And all through the night, in a bluish haze,
they move as if through a forest, among infinite houses.

CESARE PAVESE
translated from the Italian
by Geoffrey Brock

WRITING CLASS

The student all the way down
at the end of the long table said—
"If you were *my* father you'd
drive me crazy." "Why?" I thought
to myself, what have I done
to her to...oh, well. Then
I left the room to copy
a Lowell essay on freedom
in poetry while the students wrote
and on the way back
remembered the story
about her cop father's pink
Harley, and about how much
she loved him. But something else
kept coming into my mind,
though I still can't find the words—
Isn't it strange how we resent
or fear another's mind sometimes?
It's like hating the weather
because it's cold or glary,
or like not having money,
enough to buy a dress you want
or an expensive suit—
maybe why he chose pink
and how it feels to ride the thing
wide open without one thought
was the "something else." We sit
thirty feet apart. We write.
The table's cluttered with white sheets.
Head down, I hear
ballpoints rolling against wood,

maybe even a faint roar
from her old man's hot exhaust,
surely its bleak equivalent
all alone all alone

STEPHEN BERG

WHY DO POETS WRITE?

My wife, a psychiatrist, sleeps
through my reading and writing in bed,
the half-whispered lines,
manuscripts piled between us,

but in the deep part of night
when her beeper sounds
she bolts awake to return the page
of a patient afraid he'll kill himself.

She sits in her robe in the kitchen,
listening to the anguished voice
on the phone. She becomes
the vessel that contains his fear,

someone he can trust to tell
things I would tell to a poem.

RICHARD JONES

IN HIDING

I look at the mountain from the window,
it does not see me.
I hide, I write a poem,
not that it matters,
and I see the old grace. It is useless.
As before, the moon cuts into the sky
and the cherry opens.

May 9, 1944

MIKLÓS RADNÓTI
translated from the Hungarian
by Stephen Berg, S. S. Marks,
and Steven Polgar

A WOMAN WRITER DOES LAUNDRY

Enough typing.
Today I am doing laundry
in the old style.
I wash, I wash, rinse, wring
as did my grandmothers and great-grandmothers.
Relaxation.

Doing laundry is healthful and useful
like a washed shirt. Writing
is suspect.
Like three interrogation marks
typed on a page.

ANNA SWIR
translated from the Polish
by Czeslaw Milosz and
Leonard Nathan

"TO WRITE MORE"

To write more. To speak more. To whom?
How? Why? What sense does it make? Soon
we may be forced into silence. Soon
we may be forced to speak more
and more loudly. Who knows. But what
remains unspoken is always the most important:
this little man, this child, this
word, thought, and look of a child
deep inside you, you must guard,
you must defend and cherish.
And with it you will learn to speak,
and with it you will learn to be silent
if you must.

JAAN KAPLINSKI
translated from the Estonian
by Jaan Kaplinski,
Riina Tamm, and
Sam Hamill

LEARNING A DEAD LANGUAGE

There is nothing for you to say. You must
Learn first to listen. Because it is dead
It will not come to you of itself, nor would you
Of yourself master it. You must therefore
Learn to be still when it is imparted,
And, though you may not yet understand, to remember.

What you remember is saved. To understand
The least thing fully you would have to perceive
The whole grammar in all its accidence
And all its system, in the perfect singleness
Of intention it has because it is dead.
You can learn only a part at a time.

What you are given to remember
Has been saved before you from death's dullness by
Remembering. The unique intention
Of a language whose speech has died is order
Incomplete only where someone has forgotten.
You will find that that order helps you to remember.

What you come to remember becomes yourself.
Learning will be to cultivate the awareness
Of that governing order, now pure of the passions
It composed; till, seeking it in itself,
You may find at last the passion that composed it,
Hear it both in its speech and in yourself.

What you remember saves you. To remember
Is not to rehearse, but to hear what never
Has fallen silent. So your learning is,
From the dead, order, and what sense of yourself
Is memorable, what passion may be heard
When there is nothing for you to say.

W.S. Merwin

CALIFORNIA

for Adrienne Rich

To come again into the place of revolutionary
thought after years in the wilderness
of complacency and hard-eyed greed
and brutality
is extraordinary. A.'s kitchen
in Santa Cruz
isn't greatly different from her kitchen in
West Barnet in the old days,
small interesting ornaments here and there,
many good things to eat—
and how ideas flew from stove to table,
from corner to corner. In Santa Cruz
after twenty-odd years it was the same. Tolstoi said
the purpose of poetry is to provoke
feeling in the reader, to "infect" the reader,
he said,—and so to induce a change,
a change of conscience
that may lead to a change in the world, that will
lead to a change in the world!
How can poetry be written by people who want no change?

To be reconciled after so long,
in sunshine, among Latino voices. A. showed me
where earthquake two years ago had changed Santa Cruz
and how the people were rebuilding, making it better. Had she
been frightened? Of course. Would she move away?
Never. Here earth itself gives us the paradigm.
And the great ocean hurling its might always thunderously against
the land at Half Moon Bay is our measure
of flux and courage
and eternity.

We drove among hills, redwood and eucalyptus,
dense growth, the richness and ramifying intricacy
of the world's loveliness, and asked
what would be left
for our grandchildren, already born, when they are
as old as we? No longer do we
need an insane president to end us
by pushing a button. People
need only go on living as they are, without change,
the complacent and hard-eyed
everywhere. At the airport
after dark
among hard lights
with the massive proportions of human energy
surrounding them, two old people
embraced in love of the injured and poor, of poetry,
of the world in its still remaining remote possibilities,
which were themselves.

HAYDEN CARRUTH

BY THE RIVERS

That spring he was fourteen,
sun on the walls, stale air
sweet in Bergen-Belsen for the first time,
he told me he thought of the nurse
who held him when he was small.
He found a corner
where they did not catch him:
rush of the brilliance and the heat
and no one there. He opened his clothes,
hunched over his wasted body,
and made it spill.

*

The poem wants to look forward, not
back, but out there as far as it can see
are ruins: body of Abel body of god body
of smoke. And no recognizable
child to mourn.

So it begins with longing.
Or with fear, that old dog
stinking beside it, scabby and blind.

And all the time the future
is pushing up uncalled for
under the cold ground, or gliding down
like the first snow, wet syllables
that melt and soak up the darkness.

The poem wants to get out of
where it is. But is instructed
to remember. In shameless daylight.
By the rivers of salt.

SHIRLEY KAUFMAN

AFTER OUR WAR

After our war, the dismembered bits
—all those pierced eyes, ear slivers, jaw splinters,
gouged lips, odd tibias, skin flaps, and toes—
came squinting, wobbling, jabbering back.
The genitals, of course, were the most bizarre,
inching along roads like glowworms and slugs.
The living wanted them back but good as new.
The dead, of course, had no use for them.
And the ghosts, the tens of thousands of abandoned souls
who had appeared like swamp fog in the city streets,
on the evening altars, and on doorsills of cratered homes,
also had no use for the scraps and bits
because, in their opinion, they looked good without them.
Since all things naturally return to their source,
these snags and tatters arrived, with immigrant uncertainty,
in the United States. It was almost home.
So, now, one can sometimes see a friend or a famous man talking
with an extra pair of lips glued and yammering on his cheek,
and this is why handshakes are often unpleasant,
why it is better, sometimes, not to look another in the eye,
why, at your daughter's breast thickens a hard keloidal scar.
After the war, with such Cheshire cats grinning in our trees,
will the ancient tales still tell us new truths?
Will the myriad world surrender new metaphor?
After our war, how will love speak?

JOHN BALABAN

AUGUST 22, 1939

> *"...when you want to distract your mother from the discouraging soulness, I will tell you what I used to do. To take her for a long walk in the quiet country, gathering wildflowers here and there, resting under the shade of trees, between the harmony of the vivid stream and the tranquillity of the mother-nature, and I am sure she will enjoy this very much, as you surely will be happy for it. But remember always, Dante, in the play of happiness, don't use all for yourself only, but down yourself just one step, at your side and help the weak ones that cry for help, help the prosecuted and the victim; because they are your friends; they are the comrades that fight and fall as your father and Bartolo fought and fell yesterday, for the conquest of the joy of freedom for all and the poor workers. In this struggle of life you will find more love and you will be loved."*
>
> —Nicola Sacco to his son Dante, August 18, 1927
>
> *Angst und Gestalt und Gebet*
>
> —Rilke

What is it all for, this poetry,
This bundle of accomplishment
Put together with so much pain?
Twenty years at hard labor,
Lessons learned from Li Po and Dante,
Indian chants and gestalt psychology;
What words can it spell,
This alphabet of one sensibility?
The pure pattern of the stars in orderly progression,
The thin air of fourteen-thousand-foot summits,
Their Pisgah views into what secrets of the personality,

The fire of poppies in eroded fields,
The sleep of lynxes in the noonday forest,
The curious anastomosis of the webs of thought,
Life streaming ungovernably away,
And the deep hope of man.
The centuries have changed little in this art,
The subjects are still the same.
"For Christ's sake take off your clothes and get into bed,
We are not going to live forever."
"Petals fall from the rose,"
We fall from life,
Values fall from history like men from shellfire,
Only a minimum survives,
Only an unknown achievement.
They can put it all on the headstones,
In all the battlefields,
"Poor guy, he never knew what it was all about."
Spectacled men will come with shovels in a thousand years,
Give lectures in universities on cultural advances, cultural lags.
A little more garlic in the soup,
A half-hour more in bed in the morning,
Some of them got it, some of them didn't;
The things they dropped in their hurry
Are behind the glass cases of dusky museums.
This year we made four major ascents,
Camped for two weeks at timberline,
Watched Mars swim close to the earth,
Watched the black aurora of war
Spread over the sky of a decayed civilization.
These are the last terrible years of authority.
The disease has reached its crisis,
Ten thousand years of power,
The struggle of two laws,
The rule of iron and spilled blood,
The abiding solidarity of living blood and brain.

They are trapped, beleaguered, murderous,
If they line their cellars with cork,
It is not to still the pistol shots,
It is to insulate the last words of the condemned.
"Liberty is the mother
Not the daughter of order."
"Not the government of men
But the administration of things."
"From each according to his ability,
Unto each according to his needs."
We could still hear them,
Cutting steps in the blue ice of hanging glaciers,
Teetering along shattered arêtes.
The cold and cruel apathy of mountains
Has been subdued with a few strands of rope
And some flimsy iceaxes,
There are only a few peaks left.
Twenty-five years have gone since my first sweetheart.
Back from the mountains there is a letter waiting for me.
"I read your poem in the New Republic.
Do you remember the undertaker's on the corner,
How we peeped in the basement window at a sheeted figure
And ran away screaming? Do you remember?
There is a filling station on the corner,
A parking lot where your house used to be,
Only ours and two other houses are left.
We stick it out in the noise and carbon monoxide."
It was a poem of homesickness and exile,
Twenty-five years wandering around
In a world of noise and poison.
She stuck it out, I never went back,
But there are domestic as well as imported
Explosions and poison gases.
Dante was homesick, the Chinese made an art of it,
So was Ovid and many others,

Pound and Eliot amongst them,
Kropotkin dying of hunger,
Berkman by his own hand,
Fanny Baron biting her executioners,
Makhno in the odor of calumny,
Trotsky, too, I suppose, passionately, after his fashion.
Do you remember?
What is it all for, this poetry,
This bundle of accomplishment
Put together with so much pain?
Do you remember the corpse in the basement?
What are we doing at the turn of our years,
Writers and readers of the liberal weeklies?

KENNETH REXROTH

WHAT ISSA HEARD

Two hundred years ago Issa heard the morning birds
singing sutras to this suffering world.

I heard them too, this morning, which must mean,

since we will always have a suffering world,
we must also always have a song.

DAVID BUDBILL

DRINKING ALONE ON A SPRING NIGHT

Having indulged in a spring dream, I sober up at dawn—
To see the bright moon above a branch of plum blossom.
At last I've made up my mind to lead a simple, carefree life:
I'd rather buy a set of classics than fertile patches of land.

AN JUNG-SŎP
translated from the Chinese
by Sung-Il Lee

WORD DRUNK

I think of the twenty thousand poems of Li Po
and wonder, do words follow me or I them—
a word drunk?
I do not care about fine phrases,
the whoring after honor,
the stipend, the gift, the grant—
but I would feed on an essence
until it yields to me my own dumb form—
the weight raw, void of intent;
to see behind the clarity of my glass
the birth of new creatures
suffused with light.

JIM HARRISON

EPIPHANY

Sometimes you show yourself
and in the moment when I turn
toward your image
                                        you disappear.
Where do you go?
Where are you hiding
all this time lost in returning?
You come in dreams
and when memory tries to capture you
                                                                        I awake.
Only your eyes stay for a moment.
And to hold them:
all these labors night and day.

ELSA CROSS
translated from the Spanish
by Margaret Sayers Peden

A PHYSICS OF SUDDEN LIGHT

This is just about light, how suddenly
One comes upon it sometimes and is surprised.

In light, something is lifted.
That is the property of light,

And in it one weighs less.
A broad and wide leap of light

Encountered suddenly for a moment —
You are not where you were

But you have not moved. It's the moment
That startles you up out of dream.

But the other way around: It's the moment, instead,
That startles you into dream, makes you

Close your eyes—that kind of light, the moment
For which, in our language, we have only

The word *surprise,* maybe a few others,
But not enough. The moment is regular

As with all the things regular
At the closing of the twentieth century:

A knowledge that electricity exists
Somewhere inside the walls;

That tonight the moon in some fashion will come out;
That cold water is good to drink.

The way taste slows a thing
On its way into the body.

Light, widened and slowed, so much of it: It
Cannot be swallowed into the mouth of the eye,

Into the throat of the pupil, there is
So much of it. But we let it in anyway,

Something in us knowing
The appropriate mechanism, the moment's lever.

Light, the slow moment of everything fast.
Like hills, those slowest waves, light,

That slowest fire, all
Confusion, confusion here

One more part of clarity: In this light
You are not where you were but you have not moved.

ALBERTO RÍOS

WRITING THE POEM

Trying for some
Clean economy

These are things I left out...

The arduous journey, the drifts
The boots, the pain;
Any discussion of Death.

What was left was hope
For essence of
Movement, of cold;
Of emptiness and loss.

The idea, lean
As a needle
Sharp as the edge
Of shadow

Trying to close with
That thing straining toward me
The ultimate openness
The poem without words
The indelible thing itself

GARY HOLTHAUS

HOMAGE TO THE *WORD-HOARD*

Lord help me but my mind's a blank today, only a few words
bubbling up, words like "no," or "glum," or "dull," but there must
be thousands of others down there, rattling their cages, clamoring
to get out, all kinds of words, big ones, scrawny ones, heroic and
muscular ones, coy, loony words, words tasting of cloves and
licorice, cross-dressed words wearing feathery boas, quantum
words, kaons and koans, singularities, black hole words sucking up
light, love, and loss, exploding words, supernovas, words like
wormholes into other worlds, ancient words, Neanderthal words
rubbing together to make fire, Cro-Magnon words rubbing
together to make magic, spells, incantations to sail the dead off to
the underworld, words that make the blind see, that make the lame
walk, words queuing in iambs, *vers libre* words playing tennis
without a net, and yes, I must admit it, bad words, embarrassing
words, words I dare not mention, and ugly words, too, words with
blackheads, wens, squatty warts sprouting tufts of stiff hairs,
blubbery words, Jean-Paul Sartre words dripping *ennui,* words
smoking a cigarette, raising a Marlene Dietrich eyebrow and looking
down from a great height, words you wouldn't be caught dead
wearing, virgin words, cocky words, sluttish words, whispered-
in-the-ear words, Etruscan words, words from lost tongues, words
with fur and teeth, wolf words wandering the plain bringing down
antelope, words that singe, sing, and burn, words that calm and
soothe, grunt words, snarls, guttural words, vocables and syllables,
words like the sound of doves murmuring in immemorial elms,
words crackling like fire, big sky words, cloud words, the clumsy
words of first love, words like lucre, like treasure, wedding words,
the keening words at gravesides, healing words, words tumbling
down in a waterfall of long golden hair, words you could climb,
words turning a toad to a prince, Stonehenge words, words lost in
the pit at Chichén Itzá, sweet Words run softly till I end my song,
these words I have shored against my ruins, words I would kneel

down before, all the way down, touching my forehead to the floor,
words like a guillotine, unswerving, absolute, words to keep from
going under, from breathing the dark waters, waiting words, maybe
a ship will pass by, an island will rise up, maybe this will be the day
I crawl ashore and you will see my wordprints in the sand leading
toward the jungle—*there*—the fronds rustling, closing behind where
I have disappeared into a new world, a luminous existence,
a world so perfect there's no purpose for a poem, no need for words.

JOSEPH STROUD

THE BOOK OF QUESTIONS #XXI

And when light was forged
did it happen in Venezuela?

Where is the center of the sea?
Why do waves never go there?

Is it true that the meteor
was a dove of amethyst?

Am I allowed to ask my book
whether it's true I wrote it?

PABLO NERUDA
translated from the Spanish
by William O'Daly

FROM MY NOTEBOOK

1

Not marble hard and enduring,
not music or painting,
but the word in time.

2

Song and story are poetry.
A live story is sung
told by its melody.

3

The soul creates its banks,
mountains of ash and lead,
small copses of spring.

4

All imagery
not springing from the river
is cheap jewelry.

5

Choose poor rhyme,
undefined assonance.
When the song tells nothing
maybe the rhyme is lame.

6

Free verse, free verse . . .
Better to be free of verse
when it enslaves.

7

Rhymes verbal and weak
and temporal are strong.
Adjective and noun
are still pools of clear water,
are accidents of a verb
in the lyric grammar
of today that will be tomorrow,
of yesterday that is still.

ANTONIO MACHADO
translated from the Spanish
by Willis Barnstone

HACEDOR

After a lifetime of leaning over his guitar,
Segovia offered this aesthetic of craft: *Not more,*
not less. When approaching the romance of spirit,
Put on the brakes. Too much music, isn't music.
Be calm. Let the word do its work. Allow
each string its resonance in silence.

JOSEPH STROUD

THEORY AND PRACTICE IN POETRY

for Annie, working the desk at the Canyon Ranch

The idea that freezes me this time
is the "ideal" of a poet finding
her poetics. While outside, Mr. T
in his T-shirt is prowling the greens,
and the long lazy days are lying down
in the meadow outside the ruined
precincts of an old sophistry, in
another state, getting on toward noon,
where, among a thickness of flowers
so redolent and sweet as to dizzy
even the bees, summer slides in,
bringing a haze of heat like the skin
shed by a river when a mist rises
from its indolent wet back, droplets
of water (each carrying a world)
that travel on the back of a sequined
wind to that meadow woven of
grass, flowers, and guesswork—so
intricate a tapestry of greens
that in all that steam, and heat, and
growing matter, the *ideal of a poet*
finding her poetics is lost like
a ball in tall weeds, and the dog who
finds it carries it off in his mouth,
coating it with his sweet saliva,
and brings it, across miles of odd
synapses and scattered thoughts,
and drops it at the feet of a woman
who is staring down a well, but
just then turns away to acknowledge

the warm breath on her knee, and
reaches down and pats the warm
furred head of the panting, eager
dog, who feels pleased at his
feat of fetching, as does she, as
she rubs behind his ears
and lifting the sticky ball from
his mouth, she thinks for a minute
of tossing it down the well, but
instead she throws it, as far
as she can, into the lucid blue
desert sky, and watches
as it makes that beautiful arc
(gravity's rainbow) back
toward the sandy earth
as the dog hurtles off after it,
until, all at once, all unaware
of how he has found it—there it is: bright
and round in his mouth, then dropped
like the world at your feet.

ELEANOR WILNER

LOADING A BOAR

We were loading a boar, a goddam mean big sonofabitch and he jumped out of the pickup four times and tore out my stockracks and rooted me in the stomach and I fell down and he bit John on the knee and he thought it was broken and so did I and the boar stood over in the far corner of the pen and watched us and John and I just sat there tired and Jan laughed and brought us a beer and I said, "John it aint worth it, nothing's going right and I'm feeling half dead and haven't wrote a poem in ages and I'm ready to quit it all," and John said, "shit, young feller, you aint got started yet and the reason's cause you trying to do it outside yourself and aint looking in and if you wanna by god write pomes you gotta write pomes about what you know and not about the rest and you can write about pigs and that boar and Jan and you and me and the rest and there aint no way you're gonna quit," and we drank beer and smoked, all three of us, and finally loaded that mean bastard and drove home and unloaded him and he bit me again and I went in the house and got out my paper and pencils and started writing and found out John he was right.

DAVID LEE

IMPERFECT POETRY AND MEANINGLESS POETRY

Perfectly tired
of being caught perfectly
in fiction that is perfection,
I try to write imperfect poetry with perfect imperfection;
but I can only write imperfect poetry
imperfectly.

Fed up
with meaningful poetry,
I try to write
meaningless poetry,
but
nothing can be more difficult
than writing meaningless poetry.
Words have meaning—
infinite meaning—and meaning multiplies, multiplies;
words counterblow,
never ceasing to insist
meaninglessly
that they cannot help meaning by any means.

IIJIMA KOICHI
translated from the Japanese
by Naoshi Koriyama and
Edward Lueders

TO NO ONE IN PARTICULAR

Whether you sing or scream,
the process is the same.
You start, inside yourself,
a small explosion, the difference
being that in the scream
the throat is squeezed so that
the back of the tongue
can taste the brain's fear.
Also, spittle and phlegm
are components of the instrument.
I guess it would be possible
to take someone by the throat
and give him a good beating.
All the while, though, some fool
would be writing down the notes
of the victim, underscoring
this phrase, lightening this one,
adding a grace note and a trill
and instructions in one of those languages
revered for its vowels.
But all the time, it's consonants
coming from the throat.
Here's the one you were throttling,
still gagging out the guttural *ch*—
the throat-clearing, Yiddish *ch*—
and other consonants spurned by
opera singers and English teachers.
He won't bother you again.
He'll scrape home to take it out
on his wife, more bestial consonants
rising in pitch until spent.
Then he'll lock a leg over her

and snore, and all the time
he hasn't said a word we can repeat.
Even though we all speak his language.
Even though the toast in our throats
in the morning has a word for us—
not at all like bread in rain,
but something grittier in something
thicker, going through what we are.
Even though we snort and sniffle,
cough, hiccup, cry and come
and laugh until our stomachs turn.
Who will write down this language?
Who will do the work necessary?
Who will gag on a chicken bone
for observation? Who will breathe perfectly
under water? Whose slow murder
will disprove for all time
an alphabet meant to make sense?
Listen! I speak to you in one tongue,
but every moment that ever mattered to me
occurred in another language.
Starting with my first word.
To no one in particular.

MARVIN BELL

ARS POETICA: A STONE SOUP

There's the obese three-quarters moon of Aquinas
obsessed with a burning crescent
that will, within days, complete it! There's
the very confidence of stone soup
offered, in a gentlemanly contract,
to the dead farmer's wife.

And, here, the mean ratio of all other
ingredients (leeks, venison, potatoes, beans,
net of spices, and whole cream)
must not outweigh the beggar's alchemical
contribution of the worn limestone weight,

yes, that simple stone
bearing, at the least, something
of the salt of a long-dead sea.

There are those who, in my poor homily, will
leave the table pleased
with the wisdom and generosity of the widow:

her shared meal, his clump
of wildflowers, the springwater he brought
from the next county, and a heavy salt almost of history;
others, of course, leave the table feeling cheated—
mistaking the sum of the parts, even
the absence of carrots,
for a mysteriously minor whole.

To rescue these sad calculators from themselves
and from any suggestion
of a secret vulgarity in my poem
(as if it were my burden to welcome them
to the simple loss of all excuse),

I'll quote my friend, the poet Marvin Bell,
"Every poem is an ars poetica."

What else?

NORMAN DUBIE

THE IMPOSSIBLE INDISPENSABILITY OF THE ARS POETICA

But of course the poem is not an assertion. Do you see? When I
wrote
That all my poems over the long years before I met you made you
come true,
And that the poems for you since then have made you in yourself
become more true,
I did not mean that the poems created or invented you. How many
have foundered
In that sargasso! No, what I have been trying to say
Is that neither of the quaint immemorial views of poetry is
adequate for us.
A poem is not an expression, nor is it an object. Yet it somewhat
partakes of both. What a poem is
Is never to be known, for which I have learned to be grateful. But the
aspect in which I see my own
Is as the act of love. The poem is a gift, a bestowal.
The poem is for us what instinct is for animals, a continuing and
chiefly unthought corroboration of essence
(Though thought, ours and the animals', is still useful).
Why otherwise is the earliest always the most important, the
formative? The Iliad, the Odyssey, the Book of Genesis,
These were acts of love, I mean deeply felt gestures, which
continuously bestow upon us
What we are. And if I do not know which poem of mine
Was my earliest gift to you,
Except that it had to have been written about someone else,
Nevertheless it was the gesture accruing value to you, your essence,
while you were still a child, and thereafter
Across all these years. And see how much
Has come from that first sonnet after our loving began, the one
That was a kiss, a gift, a bestowal. This is the paradigm of

fecundity. I think the poem is not
Transparent, as some have said, nor a looking-glass, as some have also said,
Yet it has almost the quality of disappearance
In its cage of visibility. It disperses among the words. It is a fluidity, a vapor, of love.
This, the instinctual, is what caused me to write "Do you see?" instead of "Don't you see?" in the first line
Of this poem, this loving treatise, which is what gives away the poem
And gives it all to you.

HAYDEN CARRUTH

WHO I WRITE FOR

I

Historians and newsmen and people who are just curious ask me,
Who am I writing for?

I'm not writing for the gentleman in the stuffy coat, or for his offended moustache, not even for the warning finger he raises in the sad ripples of music.

Not for the lady hidden in her carriage (her lorgnette sending its cold light through the windowpanes).

Perhaps I write for the people who don't read my poems. That woman who dashes down the street as if she had to open the doors for the sunrise.

Or that old fellow nodding on a bench in the little park while the setting sun takes him with love, wraps him up and dissolves him, gently, in its light.

For everyone who doesn't read my writing, all the people who don't care about me (though they care for me, without knowing).

The little girl who glances my way as she passes, my companion on this adventure, living in the world.

And the old woman who sat in her doorway and watched life and bore many lives and many weary hands.

I write for the man who's in love. For the man who walks by with his pain in his eyes. The man who listened to him. The man who looked away as he walked by. The man who finally collapsed when he asked his question and no one listened.

I write for all of them. I write, mostly, for the people who don't
read me. Each one and the whole crowd. For the breasts
and the mouths and the ears, the ears that don't listen, but
keep
my words alive.

II

But I also write for the murderer. For the man who shut his eyes
and threw himself at somebody's heart and ate death instead
of food and got up crazy.

For the man who puffed himself up into a tower of rage and then
collapsed on the world.

For the dead women and the dead children and the dying men.

For the person who quietly turned on the gas and destroyed the
whole city and the sun rose on a pile of bodies.

For the innocent girl with her smile, her heart, her sweet medallion
(and a plundering army went through there).

And for the plundering army that charged into the sea and sank.

And for those waters, for the infinite sea.

No, not infinite. For the finite sea that has boundaries almost like
our own, like a breathing thing.

(At this point a little boy comes in, jumps in the water, and the
sea, the heart of the sea, is in his pulse!)

And for the last look, the hopelessly limited Last Look, in whose
arms someone falls asleep.

Everyone's asleep. The murderer and the innocent victim, the boss
and the baby, the damp and the dead, the dried-up old fig
and the wild, bristling hair.

For the bully and the bullied, the good and the sad, the voice with
no substance
and all the substance of the world.

For you, the man with nothing that will turn into a god, who reads
these words without desire.

For you and everything alive inside of you,
I write, and write.

VICENTE ALEIXANDRE
translated from the Spanish
by Lewis Hyde

STILL ANOTHER DAY #XXVIII

So long, visitor.
Good day.
My poem happened
for you, for nobody,
for everyone.

I beg you: leave me restless.
I live with the impossible ocean
and silence bleeds me dry.

I die with each wave each day.
I die with each day in each wave.
But the day does not die—
not ever.
It does not die.
And the wave?
It does not die.

Gracias.

PABLO NERUDA
translated from the Spanish
by William O'Daly

DEDICATED TO YOU

It is the thing you do open a book
by someone you like who never knew you
you leaf through to see
which words are dedicated to you
What gives you this posthumous feeling
Well you like his work and want your name in it
like on his dance card when there were
evening dances at your grandfather's supper club
You see Miguel Hernández and Mirabai
Dickinson Ghalib and Hayden
"Don't Kill Yourself" Carlos Drummond de Andrade
but not you you wonder when you will appear
This is more than the desire to see you engraved
in stone as an original donor to the Morgan Library
or listed in your alumnae magazine
Charter Member of the President's Circle
This is the affair you had
dedication is only part of the proof
the rest is in hand-canceled
stashed in a box made of sandalwood
lined with department-store tissue
the rain presses you to find
you are there in the pantheon
You knew it
this poet born in England died in 1950
after India's Independence
when murder was breakfast cereal and people hoarded fists
your grandfather divorced your grandmother
who went for a Muslim in Bombay
no more dances at that house of cards
Therefore your mother an only child gave birth to orphans
D.C. the fifty states and Puerto Rico

You fly across the world like mail in 1968
in the bright days of war
and department store parades
This poet loves her readers
and you loved him who died before you were born

REETIKA VAZIRANI

SOUNDS OF THE RESURRECTED DEAD MAN'S FOOTSTEPS (#2)

1. Skulls

Oh, said a piece of tree bark in the wind, and the night froze.
One could not have foreseen the stoppage.
I did not foresee it, who had expected a messiah.
No one had yet dared say that he or she was it—target or savior.
In the slippage between time and the turning planet, a buildup of
dirty grease made movement difficult.
Time slowed down while events accelerated.
The slower the eye moved, the faster events went past.
The raping and pillaging over time became one unending moment.
Nazis, who would always stand for the crimes of culture, clustered
in public intersections, awaiting deliveries.
The masses would turn in the Jews.
From the officers' quarters could be heard the beautiful Schubert.
And in the camp there was the grieving tenor of the cantor.
The one rose and the other sank.
Today, one can stroll in the footsteps of those who walked single
file from this life.
Often I stand in the yard at night expecting something.
Something in the breeze one caught a scent of as if a head of hair
had passed by without a face.
Whatever happens to us from now on, it will come up from the
earth.
It will bear the grief of the exterminated, it will lug itself upward.
It will take all of our trucks to carry the bones.
But the profane tattoos have been bled of their blue by the watery
loam, additives for worms.
Often I stand in the yard with a shovel.

2. Skulls

I am the poet of skulls without why or wherefore.
I didn't ask to be this or that, one way or another, just a young
  man of words.
Words that grew in sandy soil, words that fit scrub trees and beach
  grass.
Sentenced to work alone where there is often no one to talk to.
The poetry of skulls demands complicity of the reader, that the
  reader put words in the skull's mouth.
The reader must put water and beer in the mouth, and music in
  the ears, and fan the air for aromas to enter the
  nostrils.
The reader must take these lost heads to heart.
The reader must see with the eyes of a skull, comb the missing hair
  of the skull, brush the absent teeth, kiss the lips
  and find the hinge of the tongue.
Yes, like Hamlet, the Jew of Denmark before Shakespeare seduced
  him.
It is the things of the world which rescue us from the degradations
  of the literati.
A work shirt hanging from a nail may be all the honesty we can
  handle.
I am beloved of my hat and coat, enamored of my bed, my troth
  renewed each night that my head makes its
  impression on the pillow.
I am the true paramour of my past, though my wife swoons at the
  snapshots.
Small syringe the doctor left behind to charm the child.
Colorful yarmulke that lifted the High Holy Days.

MARVIN BELL

POETIC VOICE

Where is poetry for the people?
I asked in the bookstore. They tried to sell
me a volume of Carl Sandburg. His poetry fell
open to a "two-dollar-an-hour Wop."
I slammed it shut. Who writes a poetry
for the people? Lost in the bargain bins,
Allen the Great walked up and claimed
he spoke in his mother's voice. I saw
my old friend, Mary, with my children's names
buried in her poem among the scraps of my
old letters. Now she was working on all
her relatives from Oklahoma, trying
to render their tornado fear in poetic ellipsis,
herself the whirlwind in seven veils.
Why write poetry for the people?
W.C. Williams answered, because then
you can gawk at your neighbor's wife when she
goes out in her housecoat for the morning
news. Which many are dying for lack of.
Who is a poet for the people? "I"
said Byron. "Can't you hear the rabble
calling my name in Greece?" Neruda hid
under the table. He knew this racket,
smashing into his house, *Vox Populi.*
I looked up, I saw Linda pretending
to be Tolstoy, Amy in cranky tremolo
speaking as Keats at sixty-four, Eddie
as Plato, Heidegger, Nietzsche, even
Simone Weil. Ellen as the twenty-five
million who died of the flu. All this poetry by,
for, and of the people... I speak for her,
I speak for him, for you and you and you...

REBECCA SEIFERLE

I CAN'T WRITE A POEM ABOUT CLASS RAGE

Too prosaic, didactic,
purely political, the cause lacking
a certain loftiness, unlike homelessness
or domestic abuse, those subjects
newly upholstered with the necessary,
American-style noblesse oblige.

Maybe if I were writing in
an Eastern European language with
a translator who caught all the verve
of my colloquial phrasing, writing
from a tradition that believes in options
other than the exhausted, ethical
tepidity of Art for Art's Sake,

the verbal icon spinning away
unsullied in some universal nook,
clean as Ol' Possum's toilet bowl,
that preatomic mode that's so *outre*
but keeps on spreading anyway,
then maybe I could get away with it.

But I can't write a poem about class rage.
Who likes to read about the real-
life troubles of the undistinguished poor,
a bunch of luckless, disinherited
trailer-trash folk and their relentlessly
shitty lives? Even Keats, purged of his Cockney
accent, couldn't salvage a poem out of
my best friend's nephew, a kid too broke
to buy even half a billable hour, buried

away in the county lockup of some
unheard-of-by-their-own-standards
corner of Oklahoma, falsely accused
or raping an infant since the baby's
crank-addled mother had a score to settle
with the nephew's ex-wife. That won't
melt one stick of butter with
the versifying trust-fund crowd.

So I can't write a poem about class rage
without my own (no doubt) illicit motives
being called into question, and who am I
to take such a hectoring tone, to rant,
about someone else's baby or nephew,
and where are my credentials? What makes me
think I could throw a legislator's stone?

ERIN BELIEU

COMMENT ON THIS: IN THE REAL SCHEME OF THINGS, POETRY IS MARGINAL.

All things—
the empty wine bottle under the bed,
the silver brush on the vanity,
an untended garden behind an empty house,
willow branches, a handful
of dirt thrown down in the grave—
all things flow one into another
like lines of poems that take me
to the far reaches
of myself
where I meet you.
Remember:
when Emily Dickinson said,
"I'm nobody," she spoke for us all.

RICHARD JONES

ARS POETICA

It is almost polio season. The girls

From the cigarette factories in Massachusetts
Are still visiting the northern beaches.
At midnight, the milky rubbers
In the breakers are like a familiar invasion

Of sea life.
Sitting on the rocks we watch a runner:
Weight shifted, some *tick, tick,*
Almost of intelligence—
The bone catching of balance . . .

From behind, a red-haired girl appears—
Missing a thumb on her left hand,
Breathless, she asks for a light:
A crumpled pack of Lucky Strikes
At the top of a nylon stocking;
The other leg bare, her abdomen
And breasts plastered with white sand.
Drunk, she says, "He just swam out
Past the jetty—that was twenty minutes
Ago. You think I give a damn?"

We lit the cigarette for her. Her hands
Shaking.

No moon, it took an hour
To find all her clothing,
Dropped as they ran
Down the rock shelf through dunes...
He hadn't drowned. He swam around the jetty,

Crawled to the grasses and over the granite shelf.
Gathering his clothes, he left
Her there as a joke.

Her hair was colored
That second chaste coat of red on the pomegranate.
We were eating sandwiches on the rocks.
She frightened my mother and me. My little
Sister just thought she was funny.
In thirty years I have dreamt of her twice, once
With fear and once without. I've written
This for her, and because

Twice is too often
Considering how beautiful she was.

NORMAN DUBIE

SOMEBODY CONSOLES ME WITH A POEM

Can you hear it? Somebody's reading a poem to me over the telephone,
    he's consoling me for my dead,
        for myself,
            he's promising a snowfall on my forehead,
snow on our common resting place:
    on a bed, forests, beyond the skeletons of yesterday's flowers,
and healing silence in a gentle cellar,
    where cut plum-tree logs
        will burn, blazing
there will be wine on the table,
    onion
        and bread,
otherworldly light gleaming from a sharp knife,
and on the timeless, white cellar wall
    an ant, separated from its army,
        marches toward future centuries.
Can you hear it? What he says, he says to you as well:
    with big, black wings
        don't flap into the night,
            into mourning, into soot,
you're not an angel, nor a condor,
you're a sweet country's sole dweller,
    you're mine even though you're condemned to death!
        Your bound hair tumbles down
every night to my wrist
and I turn toward the North Star
    together with your back—
Weapons may stare at us tomorrow, too,
our misled country with thistly eyes,

we will no longer need your mercy:
we've lived everything that is life,
    everything that is the worry of people who die too early—
Look: the promised snow is falling softly already,
    down to our footprints advancing in pairs.

Sándor Csoóri
translated from the Hungarian
by Len Roberts and
László Vértes

SOME PART OF THE LYRIC

Some part of the lyric wants to exclude
the world with all its chaos and grief
and so conceives shapes (a tear, a globe of dew)

whose cool symmetries create a mood
of security. Which is something all need
and so, the lyric's urge to exclude

what hurts us isn't simply a crude
defense, but an embracing of a few
essential shapes: a tear, a globe of dew.

But to what end? Are there clues
in these forms to deeper mysteries
that no good poem should exclude?

What can a stripped art reveal? Is a nude
more naked than the eye can see?
Can a tear freed of salt be a globe of dew?

And most of all—is it something we can use?
Yes, but only as long as its beauty,
like that of a tear or a globe of dew,
reflects the world it meant to exclude.

GREGORY ORR

A TAO OF POETRY
(an excerpt)

Each word carefully
tied to the next, the poem
is a net, and no
single knot is strong enough
to bear the burden alone.

Some nets are small, cast
for shrimp or herring. Some nets
are meant to hold whales.
In the ecology of
the poem, the fish is not

prey, but the surprise
catch of the day, a diamond
in the coal, a way
of awakening to something
just beyond what words can say.

SAM HAMILL

ON EXPLORATION

A hawk drops to the treetop
Like a falling cross.
The haybarn is ticking.
The Universe has everything.
That's what I like about it.
A single chubby cloud
Beelines downwind
Trying to catch up with the others.

Yellow leaves plane across the water,
Drifting the inlet.
The pond is a droozy eye.
Details tend to equal each other,
Making decisions harder.
Is polio an endangered species?
The Universe is mostly empty,
That's important;
A fractal palindrome of concentric

Emptinesses.
Is there life out there?
Are there lawns?
Columbus is famous for discovering a place
Where there were already people
Killing each other.
Nothing missing. Nothing new.

Let's pick wildflowers.
Let's take a meteor shower.
Let's live forever and let's die, too.

JAMES GALVIN

CUCINA

I.

The most beautiful order is still
A random collection
Of things insignificant in themselves:

II.

Cranberry rosettes and candied
Violets, frosted thumb plums
Sweating midday, and gingerbread
Shaped in stars and bells.

III.

A buck, doe, and fawn dunk
Apples down near the pond where
Blue heron stalks rainbows
That dart while light recedes.

IV.

Under feather comforters and tea-rose vaults,
We sleep smelling of last night's
Spices. Outside, trees shed quilted leaves.

MARTINE BELLEN

ARS POETICA

At the edge of the forest
In the middle of the darkness
There is a hand,
As cold as copper,
Like a river
Stretched over wide stones.
Despite the hard rocks
And the furious wind
I love her
Like a flock of birds
Or a mild herd come to drink
For the exquisite rage
And sleek moss of her art.
There is something about a poem
That is violent
That is just another way to die,
Each time we realize our mysteries
We are weakened.
When I am writing I often scatter
Across a lascivious empire
Of passionate flowers.
They all seem so subversive
Even the ones with all their clothes on
They are so obsessed with the minute
Implication of who they are.
I believe if there is a struggle
It should go on
Where real lovers are.
I no longer regret
That I have smelted into one piece
For the sake of this poem.

PRIMUS ST. JOHN

POETRY READING AT THE VARNA RUINS

The wind skips in from the sea
stirring poplar catkins, wooly stuff
drifting the town in flurries,
nestling like words, like poems,
as we sit in these ancient baths, listening
to poetry, the delicate thing which lasts.
Look at these ruins. Boys, silly with love,
chatted idly by the pools. Merchants,
trading amphorae of oil and Lydian dye,
muttered about profits, seas, lost ships.
Now seagulls flap and squawk
on broken walls scurfed with weeds,
with weeds and the royal poppy.
Thracian, Greek, Roman, Bulgar, Slav,
Goths, Avars, Celts, Tatars, Huns.
Only poetry lasts.
The walls crumble: Horace endures.
And Ovid saves himself from exile
where history blows off the sea
scattering catkins through rubble of empires.

JOHN BALABAN

INSTRUCTIONS TO BE LEFT BEHIND

I've included this letter in the group
to be put into the cigar box—the one
with the rubber band around it you will find
sometime later. I thought you might
like to have an example of the way in which
some writing works. I may not say anything
very important or phrase things just-so,
but I think you will pay attention anyway
because it matters to you—I'm sure it does,
no one was ever more loved than I was.

What I'm saying is, your deep attention
made things matter—made art,
made science and business
raised to the power of goodness, and sport
likewise raised a level beyond.
I am not attaching to this a photograph
though no doubt you have in your mind's eye
a clear image of me in several expressions
and at several ages all at once—which is
the great work of imagery beyond the merely
illustrative. Should I stop here for a moment?

These markings, transliterations though they are
from prints of fingers, and they from heart
and throat and corridors the mind guards,
are making up again in you the one me
that otherwise would not survive that manyness
daisies proclaim and the rain sings much of.
Because I love you, I can almost imagine
the eye for detail with which you remember
my face in places indoors and out and far-flung,

and you have only to look upward to see
in the plainest cloud the clearest lines
and in the flattest field your green instructions.

Shall I rest a moment in green instructions?
Writing is all and everything, when you care.
The kind of writing that grabs your lapels
and shakes you—that's for when you don't care
or even pay attention. This isn't that kind.
While you are paying your close kind of attention,
I might be writing the sort of thing you think
will last—as it is happening, now, for you.
While I was here to want this, I wanted it,
and now that I am your wanting me to be myself
again, I think myself right up into being
all that you (and I too) wanted to be: You.

MARVIN BELL

POEM WITHOUT MUSIC

Wherever you are, you'll know what I'm saying, and why;
only you can interpret it,
can understand my message, which is very very simple:
purity, a bit of life, a little truth, are never forgotten—
although life, truth, purity, dissolve in our hands—
listen: these words are spoken only for you, only you will grasp
them.
Some day, like this clear winter Tuesday in 1997 under pines,
you'll read these phrases, they'll resurrect a lost moment, deep as
life itself,
and this will have done its work.
When that moment, which causes me to speak,
is smothered by custom, by a screen of superficial happiness,
you'll read this oblique record, and,
since what I say provides no facts, no information,
merely hints at what we both know without actually saying it,
you'll throw it aside, it will fall next to the skein of wool you are
using up
to knit a coat for the son you will bear soon,
you'll laugh at the dreams and words that once stirred your soul.
I write as obliquely as I can so nobody penetrates the secret.
I use allusions because,
if you feel that moment has died,
nobody should hear its tune in his heart.
When you die, so has the poem.
When you forget, the poem will have ended,
like a single note scribbled in black ink on a calendar without days,
like a code you must break as long as the happiness I wanted, for
you,
dreamed of for you,
has not dropped into your lap. And so,
you'll realize oblivion erases that moment.

If there is poetry beneath my words,
only you will know it.
It ends in you because you were its beginning.
Others cannot, should not, come close to its meaning.
That's all.

JOSÉ HIERRO
translated from the Spanish
by Stephen Berg

PARABLE OF THE VOICES

Behind the heart
is a deaf musician
beating a broken
drum. He is watching
the animals leap
through the hoops of our voices.

The air is another
earth full of burrows
the animals enter
and leave through the doors
of our voices. Down through our voices
the waterbirds dive.

ROBERT BRINGHURST

RECORDING THE SPIRIT VOICES

In the hollow below the hill vaults
I have placed a recorder
on the grave of a young woman killed in a fire
and have crouched under the arm of this angel
to wait for voices,
tree frogs whirring through the blue pines,
the Ocmulgee lapping the bank at the foot of Rose Hill.

A gray moon over the Confederate graves
gleams on the water,
the white gallon jugs floating some man's trotline.
Like me, he's trying to bring things to the surface
where they don't belong.

And across the river
blue needles rasp like the voices
I heard on television,
the documented whisper of spirits, *I'm afraid here, I'm*
afraid.
So am I now
as leaves in the hollow rustle their dry tongues:
afraid to hear a woman scream from a burning house,
to record some evidence her tombstone lied,
bury the truth these angels stand on: *born* and *died.*

DAVID BOTTOMS

POEM

Late butterflies gliding through the air—

how else to begin without a mouth
full of pins? Life is more

than chrysalis. There are voices

in the earth, a vengeance you can taste
in all our crops. The monarchs

are dying out, some say whole streams

gone to rust that once meandered down
to Mexico. Our resident road

returns no more. Only children

on the sidewalk writing stories in chalk
under blue pines dusted with wings

that flutter out of their lives.

TIMOTHY LIU

ARS POETICA

Six monarch butterfly cocoons
clinging to the back of your throat—

you could feel their gold wings trembling.

You were alarmed. You felt infested.
In the downstairs bathroom of the family home,
gagging to spit them out—
and a voice saying *Don't, don't*—

DANA LEVIN

GOING BACK TO THE CONVENT

This time it is no dream. After twenty-three years away
I wake in a Spokane convent in my Black Watch
plaid pajamas—daybreak, the last
day of September 1996. I used to spring from bed
at the bell's first clang. Now there's
something wrong with the bedsprings
I cannot fix.

Shyly, light enters, spills over
the floor of the room. Holy or not, I
feel more at home than in thirty-eight
years I lived here. Then let me admit the light,
endorse the mirror over my private
sink. Time to reopen the old account
stored in the memory bank.

What was I running from
or into? The uneasy light of the senior
prom? Mother's dream of a child bride, supported by
pennies from heaven? Or was it the writing
life laid as a sacrifice to a jealous god
on the tomb of the woman
I'd hoped to become?

Whatever it was, it will soon
be over. I write this now to reclaim it.

MADELINE DEFREES

69

If you're still and never speak
what will posterity have to relate
if you hide in the woods and swamps
how will your wisdom reveal itself
withering isn't healthy
wind and frost bring early ills
a clay ox plowing a rocky field
will never see a harvest day

HAN SHAN
(COLD MOUNTAIN)
translated from the Chinese
by Red Pine

POETS

Poets, minor or major, should arrange to remain slender,
Cling to their skeletons, not batten
On provender, not fatten the lean spirit
In its isolated cell, its solitary chains.
The taut paunch ballooning in its network of veins
Explodes from the cumberbund. The hardening artery of neck
Cannot be masked by turtle-throated cashmere or foulard of mottled silk.

Poets, poets, use rags instead; use rags and consider
That Poe did not lie in the morgue swathed
Beyond recognition in fat. Consider on this late March
Afternoon, with violet and crocus outside, fragile as glass,
That the music of Marianne Moore's small polished bones
Was not muffled, the score not lost between thighs as thick as bass-fiddles
Or cat-gut muted by dropsy. Baudelaire did not throttle on corpulence,
Rimbaud not strangle on his own grease. In the unleafed trees, as I write,
Birds flicker, lighter than lace. They are the lean spirit,
Beaks asking for crumbs, their voices like reeds.

William Carlos Williams sat close, close to the table always, always,
Close to the typewriter keys, his body not held at bay by a drawbridge of
flesh
Under doctor's dress, no gangway to lower, letting the sauces,
The starches, the strong liquor, enter and exit
With bugles blowing. Over and over he was struck thin
By the mallet of beauty, the switchblade of sorrow, died slim as a gondola,
Died curved like the fine neck of a swan.

These were not gagged, strangled, outdone by the presence
Of banquet selves. They knew words make their way through
navel and pore,
Move weightless as thistle, as dandelion drift, unencumbered.

Death happens to fatten on poets' glutted hearts. ("Dylan!"
Death calls, and the poet scrambles drunk and alone to what were once
swift, bony feet,
Casting a monstrous shadow of gargantuan flesh before he crashes.)

Poets, remember your skeletons. In youth or dotage, remain as
light as ashes.

KAY BOYLE

POETS

It is the nature of poets
to believe that they are

great (or will become great)
that their lines will echo

down the ages and be studied
by schoolchildren   but this

is statistically unlikely
the latest figures from the

NEA estimate that there are
about 100,000 more or less

literate poets in the USA
(of whom 10% are graduates

of creative writing courses)
I think my favorite of all

these poets is a young man
I met in Santa Fe   he played

the role of a poet because he
felt like a poet but he never

took the risk of writing a
single poem   his life was

his poetry and he was happy.

JAMES LAUGHLIN

EARLY SPRING EAST OF TOWN

The best time for a poet is when spring is new
when willows turn gold but not completely
if you wait until the Royal Woods look like brocade
everyone will be out gawking at flowers

YANG CHU-YUAN
translated from the Chinese by
Red Pine

I KNOW HOW EVERY POET

feels about his new poem
(and usually every poem)

it's the best he ever
wrote and better than

anybody else's rush it
off to a magazine the

presses are waiting they
say there are a hundred

thousand poets writing
in the USA (maybe more)

and if each one writes
at least one poem a week

that's a lot of diffused
satisfaction but Horace

was smarter he put his
new poems in a trunk

and left them there for
seven years or so he said

but I don't believe him.

JAMES LAUGHLIN

BRAIDED CREEK
(an excerpt)

The rabbit is born
prepared for listening,
the poet just for talk.

*

When a hammer sings
its head is loose.

*

Now an outlander, once a poet in N.Y.
crisscrossing Gotham for food and drink,
the souls of Lorca and Crane a daily solstice.

*

Strange world indeed:
a poet keeping himself awake
to write about insomnia.

*

Is this poem a pebble,
or a raindrop coated with dust?

*

Let go of the mind, the thousand blue
story fragments we tell ourselves
each day to keep the world underfoot.

JIM HARRISON AND
TED KOOSER

AN INTRODUCTION TO MY ANTHOLOGY

Such a book must contain—
it always does!—a disclaimer.
I make no such. For here
I have collected all the best—
the lily from the field among them,
forget-me-nots and mint weed,
a rose for whoever expected it,
and a buttercup for the children
to make their noses yellow.

Here is clover for the lucky
to roll in, and milkweed to clatter,
a daisy for one judgment,
and a violet for when he loves you
or if he loves you not and why not.
Those who sniff and say no,
these are the wrong ones (and
there always are such people!)—
let them go elsewhere, and quickly!

For you and I, who have made it this far,
are made happy by occasions
requiring orchids, or queenly arrangements
and even a bird-of-paradise,
but happier still by the flowers of
circumstance, cattails of our youth,
field grass and bulrush. I have included
the devil's paintbrush
but only as a peacock among barn fowl.

MARVIN BELL

THEY SAY

In Korea they say
The crow has twelve
Notes, none of them
Music—not surely.
And here, early,
A pine thrush
Sang when it felt
Hunger—invited
Nowhere its
Music came down
Heavily on wish.

In substance
I side with the crow
Whose sound
Is borne heavily—
Because the notes
Are not music,
Because the crow's
Satori
Is a mistake,
Singing that way
To pure, endless joy.

STEPHEN KUUSISTO

FOR THE SEVENTH DAY

I write this swishing poem for you,
come soon if you can,
don't wait until tomorrow night.
For the seventh day I've been staring at the stone-dead
sandhills
from this bleak hotel, and at the bored little forest.
A huge crow eats the snow in it,
patters, hawks, then soars away aslant,
northward. As if a black lump of flesh
tore out of me, taking wing.
I don't want to stare, alone, at the clock anymore,
at the bread, the knife, the body's
abruptly risen, dark craters.
Some irrepressible, earthly whisper
is about to speak with my mouth again,
and I don't want
to have faith in myself alone anymore.
Come soon if you can, a cold wind blows here
at the border of the country;
my hands are cold without you,
like the hands of a soldier standing sentry duty.

SÁNDOR CSOÓRI
translated from the Hungarian
by Len Roberts

POEMS

When you come back to me
it will be crow time
and flycatcher time,
with rising spirals of gnats
between the apple trees.
Every weed will be quadrupled,
coarse, welcoming
and spine-tipped.
The crows, their black flapping
bodies, their long calling
toward the mountain;
relatives, like mine,
ambivalent, eye-hooded;
hooting and tearing.
And you will take me in
to your fractal meaningless
babble; the quick of my mouth,
the madness of my tongue.

RUTH STONE

SINGING ALOUD

after Po Chü-I

We all have our faults. Mine is trying to write poems.
New scenery, someone I like, anything sets me off!
I hear my own voice going on, like a god or an oracle,
That cello-tone, intuition. That bell-note of wisdom!

And I can't get rid of the tempting tic of pentameter,
Of the urge to impose a form on what I don't understand,
Or that which I have to transform because it's too grim as it is.
But age is improving me: Now, when I finish a poem

I no longer rush out to impose it on friendly colleagues.
I climb through the park to the reservoir, peer down at my own reflection,
Shake a blossoming branch so I am covered with petals,
Each petal a metaphor...

By the time we reach middle life, we've all been deserted and robbed.
But flowers and grass and animals keep me warm.
And I remind myself to become philosophic:
We are meant to be stripped down, to prepare us for something better,

And, often, I sing aloud. As I grow older
I give way to innocent folly more and more often.
The squirrels and rabbits chime in with inaudible voices.
I feel sure that the birds make an effort to be antiphonal.

When I go to the zoo, the primates and I, in communion,
Hoot at each other, or signal with earthy gestures.
We must move farther out of town, we musical birds and animals,
Or they'll lock us up like the apes, and control us forever.

CAROLYN KIZER

POETRY READING

I'm curled into a ball
like a dog
that is cold.

Who will tell me
why I was born,
why this monstrosity
called life.

The telephone rings. I have to give
a poetry reading.

I enter.
A hundred people, a hundred pairs of eyes.
They look, they wait.
I know for what.

I am supposed to tell them
why they were born,
why there is
this monstrosity called life.

ANNA SWIR
translated from the Polish
by Czeslaw Milosz and
Leonard Nathan

THE MEANING OF LIFE

Even after a whole week full of it
Flapping,

Leather shoelaces
Untied

Those stormy petrels
My feelings

Refuse to settle down.

Friends come and then go,
Strangers take their place, or enemies...

What tempests
In a small town!

In the jammed daytime traffic

The whole switchboard's ganged up
On itself.

Has anyone got a boat?
I would sail out of all this

And you, too.

All these *explanations*
Poisoning the air like strychnine.

The doctor says one thing,
The professor says another.

I am beginning to see holes
Bigger than people, beckoning.

Each has his own story.

Sticking up in the air
Like the chewed skeletons of fish

The toothpick poles of masts
Sway around my bed,

But everywhere I go I am stalled.

Hands clutch at me like anchors
Begging me to stay still

And you want me to tell you the meaning of life!

In the middle of the night it crosses my mind like a yacht,
A pirate's lantern flickering.

I keep seeing it like a philosopher's raised eyebrow,

A firefly on a dark lawn
There where I'm struggling, huddled with all the others

The face of someone I love waving at me
One moment and then gone.

PATRICIA GOEDICKE

WAITING

After the fervor
of fists on the breast and fasting,
after the last plea slips through the heavenly gates
as they close and we've run out of things
to atone for, I want to start over.
The way my grandmother purified her heart
in the women's section.
But the rains are late, we're not forgiven,
and autumn won't come.
A few blurry showers in the north,
not in Jerusalem. No loosening.
No green rinsing of the trees.

We can't do anything
but wait. Fear sticks to our minds
like the black lice of newsprint.

The dead are so light, they don't wait,
don't have to consider what might happen.
The wind simply lifts them over.
Michael was edging off all summer,
week by week he grew lighter
until he left hardly anything behind.
A man grows small in the distance
as he unwillingly walks away, walks backwards
so we can see the little twist
of his smile. His face already taut as a mask
from which his breath trickled out.

Last week clouds came, a dark insensible mass
above the hills, but nothing fell. We wait
in front of an empty screen

when the movie is over and the next one hasn't begun.
Too dull or dazed to get out of our seats.
Someone is sweeping the refuse
in the aisles. Someone is torching
a car in the next block. Someone
is shooting into a gang of boys.
Someone is slashing open a woman with a knife.

Students at the vocational high school are printing
a book of poems. In celebration, they tell me.
Will you give us a poem?

We walked to his grave on the mountain
in a dry wind, our backs to the sun,
crossing an endless grid, hundreds
of empty plots evenly bordered with cement,
mingy homes for the homeless
waiting to be assigned.
"He will make peace… for us… "
When they finished the *Kaddish*
the men took turns and shoveled the soil back.

Autumn won't come, but the days are shorter
leaving us suddenly.
The heat never closes its eyes.
Staying up with the moths
and the souls of the lost ones
we're not really stranded. We just have to
lie here in the dark, soothed after love,
getting used to how it is.

There are black rubber masks in our closet.
When you tighten the buckles
and smooth the rubber snugly over your face
and attach the filter according to the printed instructions,

you can breathe fresh air
for about six hours. That's what they tell us.

Celebration. A poem. One of the birds
that woke me up today sang three notes
over and over. We stood on the balcony
watching them fly from the roof
and the eaves next door
in and out of the pines with their flawless wings.
It has to be one of the common birds,
you said, a bulbul or greenfinch.
It can't be a jay. They mostly screech.
Maybe a blackbird. Quick, on the branch.
Flicking its yellow beak,
it took off. One sunbird
dangled below us giving off sparks.
There were high-pitched calls
and a steady twitter. Most likely
it was a crested lark, you said,
but I can't tell you how any of them sing.

November 1990

SHIRLEY KAUFMAN

THE STORY OF THE END OF THE STORY

To keep from ending
The story does everything it can,
Careful not to overvalue
Perfection or undervalue
Perfect chance,
As I am careful not to do in telling.
By now a lot has happened:
Bridges under the water,
No time-outs,
Sinewy voices from under the earth
Braiding and going straight up
In a faint line.
I modify to simplify,
Complicate to clarify.
If you want to know your faults, marry.
If you want to know your virtues, die.
Then the heroine,
Who resembles you in certain particulars,
Precipitates the suicide
Of the author, wretchedly obscure,
Of that slim but turgid volume,
By letting slip:
Real events don't have endings,
Only the stories about them do.

JAMES GALVIN

"POETRY IS VERDANT"

Poetry is verdant—in spring
it is born from each raindrop, each
ray of light falling on the ground.
How much room do we have for them
between a morning and an evening
or upon a page in a book?
But now, in autumn when black clouds
slide low above us, brushing
high-tension pylons and crows
dozing there in the dusk, because
there is hardly day at all, the night is
two long black fingers holding day
and us in a grip so tight we barely have
room to breathe or think. Everything I write
is in spite of this weight
that comes, comes again, wanting
to plunge us into sleep,
into the dreams of decaying leaves and grassroots
and of the earth itself where
all our unthought thoughts and unborn poems hide.

JAAN KAPLINSKI
translated from the Estonian
by Jaan Kaplinski,
Riina Tamm, and
Sam Hamill

REVISIONIST POEM—OCTAVIO PAZ

The world is an invention of the spirit the spirit
Is an invention of the body the body
Is an invention of the world

THOMAS MCGRATH

DO NOT SPEAK KERESAN TO A MESCALERO APACHE

Do not speak
Keresan to a Mescalero Apache,
but cultivate
private languages;

a cottonwood
as it disintegrates into gold,
or a house
nailed into the earth:

the dirt road
into that reservation
is unmarked.

ARTHUR SZE

BECAUSE THE EYE IS A FLOWER WHOSE ROOT IS THE HAND,

the zoo raccoon lifts its food pellet,
& out of Genesis

the Flemish tapestry Eve shows
the apple is an object

instinct truculently makes Art.
Look & look on your knees in the small

yard as you work
the fallen earring (its coral

a tapestry knot)
from the knotted clover. Each green

clinging in the clover dozens
is a claim for Art, is a way for the earring

to survive as praise
for a way of looking.

DENNIS SCHMITZ

NIGHT SEASONS

Up late, reading alone,
I feed printed pages
Into the Kurzweil scanner,
An electronic reader
For the blind.

Randomly now
I take books from my shelves,
Open the mysterious volumes,
And lay them flat on the machine.
I can't say
What's coming next—
I wait in perfect silence
For the voice to begin,
This synthetic child
Reading to an old man.

The body, stalled,
Picks fragments,
Frottage,
Scraps of paper,
Whatever comes.

Pico della Mirandola,
Egyptian love poems,
Essene communes beside the Red Sea,
Paavo Haavikko's "König Harald"...

An old professor,
Bitter at the graceful way
The poets have
Of gathering terms

Inexactly,
Told me, “The poets are fools.
They read
Only in fragments.”

I’m the fool
Of the night seasons,
Reading anything, *anything.*
When daylight comes
And you see me on the street
Or standing for the bus,
Think of the Greek term
Entelechy,
Word for soul and body
Constructing each other
After dark.

STEPHEN KUUSISTO

OUR MOTHER TALKS ABOUT METAPHOR

Our mother cautions us.
Think of this, she says,
every time you turn around
certain you have lost something
afraid you have left it behind,
you have
you have.
But, she says solemnly, *you must*
not ask where it is,
pronouncing her words distinctly
so we get her meaning,
You must ask what *it is.*
She smiles.
What have you lost?
What?

SUSAN GRIFFIN

THE MOON IS A DIAMOND

Flavio Gonzales, seventy-two, made jackhammer
heads during the War; and tells me
about digging ditches in the Depression
for a dollar a day. We are busy plastering
the portal, and stop for a moment
in the April sun. His wife, sick for
years, died last January and left a
legacy—a $5,000 hospital bill.
I see the house he built at fifteen:
the *ristras* of red chili hanging
in the October sun. He sings "Paloma
Blanca" as he works, then stops,
turns: "I saw the TV photos of the
landing on the moon. But it's all
lies. The government just went out
in the desert and found a crater.
Believe me, I know, I know the moon
is a diamond."

ARTHUR SZE

ARS POETICA

this hush, my pollen—the ordinary grace in the buds.
the crowding,
my basement sorrows—salt and shadow, saying
Lucky, lucky, your tiniest sadness,
this desert of fragments,
openhanded voyage,
this urge to making a scrapbook of stars—

DANA LEVIN

AND IT CAME TO PASS

This june 3
would be different

Time to draw lines

I've grown into the family pores
and the bronchitis

Even up east
I get by saying goddamnit

Who was that masked man
I left for dead
in the shadow of mt. shadow

Who crumbles there

Not touching anything
but satin and dandelions

Not laid his eyes
on the likes of you

Because the unconnected life
is not worth living

Thorntrees overtake the spot

Hands appear to push back pain

Because no poet's death

Can be the sole author
of another poet's life

What will my new instrument be

Just this water glass
this untunable spoon

Something else is out there
goddamnit

And I want to hear it

C.D. Wright

THE AMBASSADOR

I lived on an alley where every cat and dog
in Santiago, Chile,
came to pee.
It was 1925.
I shut myself in with poetry
that carried me to the Garden of Albert Samain,
to the magnificent Henri de Régnier,
to Mallarmé's blue fan.

Nothing works better against the urine
of thousands of suburban dogs
than an imaginative crystal
with its pure essence, with light and sky:
the window of France, chilly parks
throughout which the impeccable statues
—it was 1925—
were exchanging marble shirts,
their patinas smoothed by the touch
of many elegant centuries.

On that alley, I was happy.

Long after, years later,
I returned as Ambassador to the Gardens.

The poets had already left.

And the statues did not know me.

PABLO NERUDA
translated from the Spanish
by William O'Daly

WHAT KEEPS

We live on a hillside
close to water
We eat in darkness
We sleep in the coldest
part of the house
We love in silence
We keep our poetry
locked in a glass cabinet
Some nights We stay up
passing it back and
forth
between us
drinking deep

C.D. Wright

THE WORD BETWEEN THE WORLD AND GOD

Which gods gave birth to which language?
Which language gave birth to which gods?
Which gods remembered which poems?
Which poems remembered which gods?
Which memory compelled the poet to write her first poem?
Which poem compelled the poet to remember her first memory?
Which memory broke into words without effort?
Which broken words were made whole by memory?
Which memory broke all the words in all the languages?
Which word unlocks the god hidden in the world?
Which hidden world contains the word of god?
Which hidden world have I locked away without words?
Which hidden world contains the ghost of a memory
too terrible for words?
Which words saved which souls?
Which souls gave which words to the world?
Which words said goodbye to which souls?
Which words are the last words?
Which words cross over the river of souls?

Who rescued herself with a word?
Who stole time for language?
Who encouraged language to steal?
Who taught language to be a sanctuary?
Who built a sanctuary out of words?
Who let herself listen to words hallowing the wind?
Who scooped out time in the quickening evening
by naming an eyeful of stars?

EMILY WARN

ERASING STARS

A teacher of standing, a poet, tells her class, "*Never put stars in your poems...*" and some of the students write this down. And some stop writing after a year or two. And some get married or take jobs selling pharmaceuticals. And some think *Time is in short supply* and *ex cathedra* take up parent worship.

I know a Baltic poet who draws Egyptian star charts on cocktail napkins as he answers questions. I also know a poet in Tucson, an amateur ornithologist who believes that stars influence birds. "Of course," he says, "the carbon in our brains comes from stars."

Erase stars from a page. Nothing happens. The allotropic pulse of mathematics ticks anyway. But now try putting the stars back. It can't be done. This failure has nothing to do with personal habits.

STEPHEN KUUSISTO

MORNING STAR

This isn't the end. It simply
cannot be the end. It is a road.
You go ahead coatless, light-
soaked, more rutilant than
the road. The soles of your shoes
sparkle. You walk softly
as you move further inside
your subject. It is a living
season. The trees are anxious
to be included. The car with fins
beams through countless
oncoming points of rage and need.
The sloughed-off cells
under our bed form little hills
of dead matter. If the most sidereal
drink is pain, the most soothing
clock is music. A poetry
of shine could come of this.
It will be predominantly
green. You will be allowed
to color in as much as you want
for green is good
for the teeth and the eyes.

C.D. WRIGHT

DAILY RITUAL

Daily ritual
its own vocabulary

settling accounts
targets
strategic approach
assessing

the situation the goddamn
situation

everyone arguing at once

litter of legs
little torn legs
of the latest

Taha Muhammed Ali begins
his poem

what makes me love
being alive

he sells olivewood camels
to tourists in Nazareth

his book
walks barefoot
on *coins with holes*
at their center
bullet casings
old ladies' copper rings
thrown away by their grandsons

it is called *Never Mind*

I'm not sure
what (if)
I love today
ask me next week

the world Ali says
and *dreams*

SHIRLEY KAUFMAN

AT SEVENTY-FIVE: REREADING AN OLD BOOK

My prayers have been answered, if they were prayers. I live.
I'm alive, and even in rather good health, I believe.
If I'd quit smoking I might live to be a hundred.
Truly this is astonishing, after the poverty and pain,
The suffering. Who would have thought that petty
Endurance could achieve so much?
And prayers—
Were they prayers? Always I was adamant
In my irreligion, and had good reason to be.
Yet prayer is not, I see in old age now,
A matter of doctrine or discipline, but rather
A movement of the natural human mind
Bereft of its place among the animals, the other
Animals. I prayed. Then on paper I wrote
Some of the words I said, which are these poems.

HAYDEN CARRUTH

STORIES ARE MADE OF MISTAKES

1

Even the pole bean tendrils sought out and gripped their
frames within six hours of my setting them.
One of the things
that is breaking my heart is that I can't trust language to
express any thanks.
My pole beans, my honeybees, my coyotes,
my dog, all my good horses.

2

The black mare I shouldn't have bought and bought, and once
I had, should have shipped, bucked me, too, the first time
I got up.
But God she was a beauty.
I thought if I just rode her
I could ride her down.
Her name was Sara and we kept it at that.

All she wanted to do was run.
Ears back, flat out, nose pushed
into the next life.
I wanted her to learn to walk.

3

After about a year of chop I turned her uphill on a good gravel
road and said, "OK, you bitch, you want to run?"
I let go
her head and gave her the steel.
I'd never been on a horse so
fast.
I've never been on one since.

So fast you couldn't
count the beats in the rhythm of her gait.
Suicidal.
But when,
after some miles, she started to flag, I said, "I thought you
wanted to run," and dug her out again.

4

The pole bean tendrils sought their frames within six hours
of my setting them.
They broke my heart.
They gripped.

5

A patch of sunlight mottled the shade.
Whether she never
saw the root that snaked through the shadow or was just too
far in front of herself, I'll never know.
She stumbled
and fell.
First on her knees then over.
We rasped together
down the gravel road, black mare on top of me.
We rasped
to a halt.
She jumped to her feet.
She stared at me.
I
could see the bone in both her knees.
Ribbons of hide hanging.

Blood like volunteer firemen beginning to rise to the occasion.

6

Ten years later, today, I'm riding her.
I keep her reined
in most of the time.
She tosses her head, snaps tie-downs.

She dances and whirls, doubles under and rears incessantly.

She makes me the butt of ridicule:
"So, uh, Jim, how old
is that mare?"
"She must be twenty now."
"Don't you think
it's time she was broke?"
Every once in a while I let her
run and break my heart.
Anyone watching stops breathing.

If I ever get to heaven and know who I am, I'd like to overhear my daughter tell a story to her children.
"Sometimes
my dad used to ride this black mare..."

JAMES GALVIN

DADDY OUT HITCH-HIKING AT 3:00 A.M.

Finally it was just me, and the katydids
cranking out nightsongs in clumps of willows
by a barn roofed in moonlight, by a ryefield
luminous with dew. I stepped off the highway
ribboning out through the valley. Walked
through wet weeds to a pond gathering vapors.

Angels see the way I saw that night
when only large shapes loomed
and all my thoughts were laid aside
as I searched the night opening before me
and soul shuffled out of self to sing
with katydids chattering in murky trees.

All beasts are kind with divine instruction.
The paired ducks slept beneath their wings.
Minnows wavered in the moon-charmed creek
where a muskrat hunched and licked its paws
listening like me to insects calling
searching and calling at the end of summer.

This is what Daddy was doing
the August you were born.
Wandering off alone on highways
walking off highways into the night
calming a head loud with the past
listening to things that make a song.

JOHN BALABAN

ON THIS SIDE OF THE RIVER

to Millie

Simply trust:
don't the petals also flutter down
just like that?

—Issa

I undress and lie down next to you in bed
and throw one of my legs across yours, I wait
until you are completely lost
then slide my head on the pillow with yours.
Your hair gets caught in my teeth.
I stretch a little to rub my head against yours, so
gently neither of us can feel it,
my breath goes and returns with yours.
There is a moon. Clouds streak its face.
At this late hour by the river the cherry trees stand alone,
black tongueless sentinels
that report nothing.
Wind shakes the flowers that hang over the water,
on the other side families sit down to eat.
I know it.
Not one petal has been torn loose,
and I lie here with my hands on you, not moving,
seeing us today under the trees
sitting with our legs crossed facing each other, talking,
and try to remember what we said.
Get up. I want you to explain
what no couple has ever understood—
the silence, our two skins, the fact that one dies first.
One angry face the color of the
blossoms flashes up and leaves.
The moon pours in. I begin telling you about

my life like the cabdriver in the story
who plows all night through Moscow desperate
for someone to listen to him and winds up at dawn
standing under a streetlamp, snow chilling his mouth,
telling his horse how terrible life is because his
five-year-old son died yesterday, and not one passenger
would listen,
pulling the nag's ear down to his mouth, whispering deep
into it his unbearable story.

STEPHEN BERG

THE MAGICIAN-MADE TREE
(*an excerpt*)

The Bargain

In the transatlantic fury
when I feared
I might not survive
to see Florence,
clutching an elfin
Love Sonnets of Shakespeare,
I implored:
Lord, let me live
long enough to dare
a love poem—

In time, of course, the skies
stopped glowering.
And in the Tuscan summer's imperial
segue into autumn,
poetry burgeoned—

It's not only the active grace,
the glory between us:
these praise songs spring
from a holy bargain,
from my deepest desire
to live.

Cyrus Cassells

PHOTOVOLTAIC

Lord let me all I can wild cherry
I'm dazed all my ways of arriving bear tracks
failure of being torn to pieces is me
mumbling anxiety and I love my heart
I do each day lightly suffering desire
for kindness vividly today
idiot red unselfish green blue threadbare of cloud
outside the labyrinth imagining my life

Write poems
starve off death

Isn't the earth warm
the dew stars and the whole
yours for more work perhaps
inside we change work changes

Lord the voice was large
lord the voice is large
begging even

Nurse openly and everywhere
earth hand into being
you build
we care
you cut
we perish
tearing cloth apart
you are our tusk

I had no other dream
I reported back
for this large meaning
bent this way that vernacular with me
Eden after melancholy
palms suddenly heralds

Insistent love I won't outlive the words I lamb in your mouth
anachrist of the bewildered touch of extreme hands

Empty of shit the race is on
empty of eyes made of wood with indifference
don't you straighten it
don't pretend your mouth is not on fire
that stupidity bursts the needle
absolutely on the solid floor
race for the oar light sleeps to dream
travel through shining the ration before you
for every hurt be my large palm
Poetry

OLGA BROUMAS

HOMAGE TO LIFE: JULES SUPERVIELLE

It is good to have chosen
a living home
and harbored time
in a constant heart,
to have seen one's hands
touch the world
as an apple
in a small garden,
to have loved the earth,
the moon and the sun,
like old friends
beyond any others,
and to have entrusted
the world to memory
like a luminous horseman
to his black steed,
to have given shape
to these words: wife, children,
and to have served as a shore
for roving continents
to have come upon the soul
with little oarstrokes
for it is frightened
by a sudden approach.
It is good to have known
the shade under the leaves
and to have felt age
steal over the naked body
accompanying the grief
of dark blood in our veins
and glazing its silence
with the star, Patience,

and to have all these words
stirring in the head,
to choose the least beautiful
and make a little feast for them,
to have felt life
rushed and ill-loved,
to have held it
in this poetry.

JOSEPH STROUD

THE SNOW AND THE PLUM—I

The plum and the snow both claim the spring
a poet gives up trying to decide
the plum must admit the snow is three times whiter
but the snow can't match a wisp of plum perfume

THE SNOW AND THE PLUM—II

The plum without the snow isn't very special
but snow without a poem is simply commonplace
at sunset when the poem is done then it snows again
together with the plum they complete the spring

LU MEI-P'O
translated from the Chinese
by Red Pine

COUNTRY SCENE

The waterfall plunges in mist.
Who can describe this desolate scene:

the long white river sliding through
the emerald shadows of the ancient canopy

...a shepherd's horn echoing in the valley,
fishnets stretched to dry on sandy flats.

A bell is tolling, fading, fading
just like love. Only poetry lasts.

Hồ Xuân Hương
translated from the Vietnamese
by John Balaban

THE LAST POEM IN THE WORLD

Would I write it if I could?
Bet your glitzy ass I would.

HAYDEN CARRUTH

ABOUT THE POETS AND THEIR POETRY

VICENTE ALEIXANDRE won the Nobel Prize in Literature in 1977, but his start in poetry was fairly common. At the age of 19, while living alone in a small mountain village in Spain, he discovered the poetry of the great Nicaraguan modernist Rubén Dario. The young Aleixandre had not read much poetry, but Dario's poems led him to the work of Antonio Machado and Juan Ramón Jiménez. Their poems led him to write his own, though he kept his work secret for many years. When an illness forced him to leave his job as a law professor, he returned to the mountains, where he dedicated himself to his poetry, publishing his first book at the age of thirty. His book *A Longing for the Light* was edited by Lewis Hyde, and published by Copper Canyon Press in 1985.

AN JUNG-SŎP was a nineteenth-century Korean poet who, like many other pre-twentieth-century Korean poets, wrote in Chinese. This translation by Sung-Il Lee comes from *The Moonlit Pond: Korean Classical Poems in Chinese.*

JOHN BALABAN is the author of eleven books of poetry and prose, including four volumes which together have won The Academy of American Poets' Lamont prize, a National Poetry Series Selection, and two nominations for the National Book Award. His *Locusts at the Edge of Summer: New and Selected Poems* won the 1998 William Carlos Williams Award from the Poetry Society of America. He is also a translator of Vietnamese poetry, including *Spring Essence: The Poetry of Hồ Xuân Hương,* and *Ca Dao Vietnam: Vietnamese Folk Poetry.*

ERIN BELIEU is the author of two books of poetry, *One Above & One Below* and *Infanta,* which was a National Poetry Series winner. In her two poems, "I Can't Write a Poem About Class Rage" and "Love Poem," she joins a long tradition of poets who write precisely what they supposedly are not to write about.

MARVIN BELL is the author of dozens of volumes of poetry and prose, including his most recent, *Nightworks.* He has made a life out of writing and teaching poetry, always challenging the art form. As Norman Dubie quotes him in "Ars Poetica: A Stone Soup," Bell has said that "Every poem is an ars poetica." Every poem is about poetry. During the past decade Bell has devoted himself to *The Book of the Dead Man,* a series of poems which uses the voice of the "dead man" as a way to explore the very process of creation and the notion of the self.

MARTINE BELLEN is the author of three volumes of poetry, including *The Vulnerability of Order*. Her poem "Cucina" is not only about cooking, but also is about different ways of seeing, different senses, different ways of assembling the world around us—precisely what the poet does when she creates worlds within a poem. Poems are sometimes "A random collection / of things insignificant in themselves"—like animals searching for food—sometimes they are intentionally made things, and still other times they are a combination of both.

STEPHEN BERG is the author of dozens of books of poetry and "versions." In the latter, he blurs the lines between direct word-for-word translation and the need to create poems. These versions can be a mixture of direct translation and homage, often favoring meaning over definition in an attempt to create a newly made poem instead of an impossible mirror reflection of the original. His books of versions include *Crow with No Mouth: Ikkyū* and *Steel Cricket: Versions, 1958-1997*. His poems are collected in *Selected Poems.*

DAVID BOTTOMS is the author of seven volumes of poetry, including *Armored Hearts: New & Selected Poems* and *Vagrant Grace.* His new collection, *Vigilance,* is due from Copper Canyon Press in 2004. Bottoms has his literary ancestry rooted in the literature of the American South, and he writes very much in the vein of James Dickey or Robert Penn Warren. His sources of inspiration, though, aren't entirely literary and have often included southern landscapes, family, and, as in the poem, "Recording the Spirit Voices," cemeteries.

KAY BOYLE published ten novels, a half dozen short novels, numerous short story collections, and three children's books, along with essays and several volumes of poetry. A resident of Paris for nearly twenty years before World War II, she returned to the U.S. and taught at San Francisco State University.

CORAL BRACHO lives and writes in Mexico City. Her poem "The Allure of Forms" was written in response to a painting. As with most poems about art, it speaks to more than a single subject, addressing in this instance the creation of poetic and visual forms. Her poem was translated by Mónica de la Torre and appears in *Reversible Monuments: Contemporary Mexican Poetry.*

ROBERT BRINGHURST is not only a brilliant poet, but is also one of the world's foremost typographers. Widely published in his native Canada, he has published two collections in the U.S., *The Beauty of Weapons* and *Pieces of Map, Pieces of Music.* In addition to his poetry, he is the author of *The Elements of Typographical Style.*

OLGA BROUMAS was born in Syros, Greece, in 1949 and published her first book of poems, written in Greek, in 1967. After moving to the United States she received her B.A. in architecture from the University of Pennsylvania and an M.F.A. in creative writing from the University of Oregon. Her first book in English, *Beginning with O,* won the Yale Younger Poets Award in 1977. Since then she has published five books of her own poetry, including *Rave: Poems, 1975-1999,* and has translated three volumes of poems and a volume of essays by the Greek Nobel laureate, Odysseas Elytis.

DAVID BUDBILL has been writing poems about Judevine Mountain for nearly forty years, creating a semi-fictitious, isolated mountain in Vermont where the great sages of the classical Chinese world gather. His most recent report from Judevine is *Moment to Moment.*

HAYDEN CARRUTH is the author of dozens of volumes of poetry and prose about poetry. When told about this anthology of poems about poetry he responded: *As a child of the fifties and sixties, I have had more than my fill of self-reflexive poems. I used to reject them out of hand, no matter who wrote them, and I still think this is a good idea. Nobody but giddy sophomores wants to read such poems. There are plenty of other topics, viz.*

Poems about the city.
Poems about sex.
Poems about politics.
Poems about winter.
Poems about eating and food.
Poems about physical pain.

Carruth's many books include *The Collected Shorter Poems, 1946-1991, Scrambled Eggs & Whiskey,* and most recently, *Doctor Jazz.*

CYRUS CASSELLS is the author of four books of poetry, including *Soul Make a Path Through Shouting* and *Beautiful Signor.* In addition to writing poetry, he is an actor, teaches at Southwestern Texas University, and lives in Austin, Texas.

ELSA CROSS lives in Mexico City and has been publishing her poetry consistently since the early 1960s. Her work has been widely anthologized and translated into many languages, including English in the anthology *Reversible Monuments: Contemporary Mexican Poetry.* A professor of philosophy and comparative mythology at the Universidad Nacional Autónoma de México, she has taught throughout Mexico, the United States, and Spain. Her poetry was translated by Margaret Sayers Peden.

SÁNDOR CSOÓRI is the author of dozens of volumes of poetry published in his native Hungary. Born in Zamoly, Hungary, in 1930, he has long been a political and human rights activist. His *Selected Poems* was translated by Len Roberts and László Vértes.

MADELINE DEFREES was born in Ontario, Oregon, in 1919. At age 17 she entered the convent of the Sisters of the Holy Names of Jesus and Mary, assuming the name of Sister Mary Gilbert for the next 38 years. She has published eight volumes of poetry and two memoirs of her life as a nun. Her book *Blue Dusk: New & Selected Poems, 1964-2001* was the winner of the 2002 Lenore Marshall Poetry Award.

NORMAN DUBIE is a Regents' professor at Arizona State University. A practitioner of Tibetan Buddhism whose work has been translated into thirty languages, Dubie is a highly regarded and widely anthologized poet who decided to take a decade-long hiatus from publishing his poems. He broke his silence with the publication of *The Mercy Seat: Collected and New Poems, 1967-2001,* which won the 2002 PEN Award in poetry.

JEAN FOLLAIN was born in Canisy, in Normandy, and as a law student, moved to Paris in 1925 to continue his studies. He began to practice law and eventually became a judge. In Paris his life and literary beginning were quiet. He associated with a group that included Max Jacob, Pierre Reverdy, and Léon-Paul Fargue, and his poems were published in several literary reviews. His first substantial book of poems, *La Main Chaude,* was published in 1933. He later published eight subsequent volumes of poetry. W. S. Merwin's translations of his poems appear in *Transparence of the World.*

JAMES GALVIN is the author of the highly acclaimed memoir/history of place, *The Meadow,* the novel *Fencing the Sky,* and five volumes of poetry, including *Resurrection Update: Collected Poems.* In 2002 he was awarded a Lannan Literary Fellowship. His book, *X,* will be published in 2003.

PATRICIA GOEDICKE has published twelve volumes of poetry and has earned an impressive range of recognition, including a *New York Times* Notable Book of the Year and a William Carlos Williams Award. She lives in Missoula, Montana and teaches at the University of Montana.

SUSAN GRIFFIN is a critically acclaimed feminist writer, poet, essayist, lecturer, playwright, and filmmaker. She is author of more than twenty books, including *The Eros of Everyday Life* and *Bending Home: New & Collected Poems. The Utne Reader* named her one of the "100 Visionaries Who Could Change Your Life."

HAN SHAN's name translates as "Cold Mountain." He was a Taoist/Buddhist hermit who lived 1,200 years ago in the Tientai Mountains of China. He begged for food at temples, often sang and drank with cowherds, and became an immortal figure in the history of Chinese literature and Zen. Many of his poems were written on the rocks and cliff walls surrounding the cave in which he lived. *The Collected Songs of Cold Mountain* were translated by Red Pine (Bill Porter).

SAM HAMILL is the author of a dozen volumes of poetry, two dozen translations, and numerous literary essays. His books include *Dumb Luck, Gratitude,* and *Crossing the Yellow River: Three Hundred Poems from the Chinese.* He is the founding editor of Copper Canyon Press, and for the past thirty years he has inspired, encouraged, mentored, and challenged poets, writers, and editors to follow the path of poetry.

JIM HARRISON is the author of twenty-three books, including *Legends of the Fall* and *The Shape of the Journey: New and Collected Poems,* and has served as food columnist for the magazines *Smart* and *Esquire.* His work has been translated into two dozen languages and produced as four feature-length films. His most recent volume, *Braided Creek,* is a collaboration with the poet Ted Kooser, which gathers a "correspondence in poetry" wherein the reader never knows which poet is writing which poem.

JOSÉ HIERRO was born in Madrid in 1922, yet has lived the majority of his life in Santander. One of Spain's great twentieth-century poets, he first came to fame in the 1940s and 1950s, when Spanish poetry was still marked by the famous "Generation of '27" and by the aftermath of the Spanish Civil War. He has published more than a dozen books of poetry, philosophy, and criticism. The translation of his poem appears in Stephen Berg's *The Steel Cricket: Versions, 1958–1997.*

GARY HOLTHAUS is the author of two collections of poetry, *Unexpected Manna,* and *Circling Back,* and the co-editor of *The Great Land: Reflections on Alaska, A Society to Match the Scenery,* and *AQR's Alaska Native Writers, Orators and Storytellers.* He is the former director of the Alaska Humanities Forum and current director of the Center of the American West at the University of Colorado in Boulder.

HỒ XUÂN HƯƠNG, in writing "only poetry lasts," spoke not only of the power of poetry, but of its condition in Vietnam. Many of that country's plastic arts—its sculpture, painting, printmaking, etc.—have suffered terribly from war and weather. Yet poetry, written, and more often, memorized, has managed to last through many centuries. Today, as one walks the streets of Hanoi, one will find many different volumes of the poetry of Hồ Xuân Hương, published in modern editions some two hundred years after her death. Her poems, translated by John Balaban, appear in *Spring Essence: The Poetry of Hồ Xuân Hương.*

IIJIMA KOICHI was born in Okayama City, Japan, and graduated from Tokyo University with a degree in French literature. As the author of several volumes of poetry, his work is heavily influenced by the French Surrealists and has played an important role in defining postwar Japanese poetry. His poetry, translated by Naoshi Koriyama and Edward Lueders, appears in *Like Underground Water: The Poetry of Mid-Twentieth Century Japan.*

RICHARD JONES is the author of four books of poetry, including *The Blessing: New & Selected Poems.* He is editor of *Poetry East,* teaches at DePaul University, and lives in Chicago with his wife Laura and their sons, William and Andrew.

JAAN KAPLINSKI, a linguist, ecologist, and anthropologist, is the leading poet of Estonia and one of its foremost social commentators. In recent years Kaplinski has gradually accumulated an international reputation as a poet with a radically ecological and biological message, whose view of the world is rooted in ancient Chinese philosophy, especially Taoism. His book, *The Wandering Border,* was translated by Kaplinski, Riina Tamm, and Sam Hamill.

SHIRLEY KAUFMAN is the author of seven books, including *Roots in the Air: New & Selected Poems* and the forthcoming collection *Threshold,* as well as several translations from Hebrew. A native of Seattle, Kaufman now makes her home in Jerusalem.

CAROLYN KIZER is a recipient of the Pulitzer Prize in Poetry whose poetry is gathered in *Cool, Calm, & Collected: Poems 1960-2000.* In 1959 she co-founded *Poetry Northwest* and remained its editor until 1965. She served as the first director of the Literature Program at the National Endowment for the Arts, was a chancellor of the Academy of American Poets, and has been a poet-in-residence at Columbia, Stanford, and Princeton, among many other universities. She lives in Sonoma, California.

TED KOOSER is the former vice-president of Lincoln Benefit Life, an insurance company. He is the author of ten collections of poetry, including his forthcoming "correspondence in poetry," *Braided Creek* (with Jim Harrison), and *Delights and Shadows.*

STEPHEN KUUSISTO is a spokesperson for Guiding Eyes for the Blind and teaches creative writing at Ohio State University. His best-selling memoir, *Planet of the Blind,* was named a Notable Book of the Year by *The New York Times,* and his essays and poems have appeared in *Harper's, The New York Times Magazine, Poetry,* and *Seneca Review.* His poetry book is *Only Bread, Only Light.*

JAMES LAUGHLIN was the founder, publisher, and driving force behind the most influential poetry publishing house of the twentieth century, New Directions. As a twenty-two-year-old sophomore at Harvard University he founded New Directions in 1936, and went on to publish some of this century's greatest writers: Ezra Pound, H.D., William Carlos Williams, Henry Miller, Kenneth Rexroth, Gary Snyder, and many others. As a champion of literature in translation, New Directions published Boris Pasternak, Vladimir Nabokov, Pablo Neruda, and Octavio Paz, among others. Laughlin died in 1997.

DAVID LEE is the author of *A Legacy of Shadows* and *News from Down to the Cafe,* and became Utah's first poet laureate. A former seminary candidate, semi-pro baseball player, and hog farmer, he has a Ph.D. concentration in John Milton and is the head of the Languages and Literature department at Southern Utah University. His forthcoming collection is entitled *So Quietly the Earth.*

DANA LEVIN grew up in Lancaster, California, in the Mojave Desert. Her book, *In the Surgical Theatre* won the *American Poetry Review*/Honickman First Book Prize. She teaches at the College of Santa Fe.

TIMOTHY LIU is the author of four collections of poems, including *Burnt Offerings* and *Say Goodnight,* and is the editor of *Word of Mouth: An Anthology of Gay American Poetry.* He earned degrees at Brigham Young University and the University of Houston, and currently lives and teaches in Paterson, New Jersey.

LU MEI-P'O, a poet of the Sung dynasty, has left nothing but two poems behind. The name by which he was known means Plum Slope. His translator, Red Pine (Bill Porter), writes in *Poems of the Masters* that some scholars have attributed these two poems to Fang Yueh (1199–1262). Porter writes: "Either way, they are good examples of the Chinese poets' view of their art. In the first poem, the poet demonstrates that there are no absolutes. Everything has its own unique, incomparable quality. But this leaves us with a conundrum: in a world where everything is unique, what can we use as a standard, and how can we speak of beauty? In this second verse, the poet resolves his conundrum by introducing the poem, and thus the poet, as the catalyst that transforms the separate worlds of the plum and the snow into one world of beauty. Thus, the poet justifies his existence as well as his passion by his ability to perceive the spirit and appearance of things in a world not divided by things, which is what a poem aims to do."

ANTONIO MACHADO was perhaps the most esteemed of Spain's "Generation of '98." He wrote about his beloved Spanish countryside during the years leading up to and including the Spanish Civil War. He died in the Pyrenees while fleeing Franco's fascists, with little but the coat on his back, his pockets stuffed with poems. A selection of his poems has been translated by Willis Barnstone in *Almost Naked, Like the Children of the Sea.*

CLARENCE MAJOR is the author of dozens of books of poetry, fiction, and nonfiction, including *Waiting for Sweet Betty* and *Configurations: New & Selected Poems, 1958-1998,* which was a finalist for the 1999 National Book Award. In addition to being a writer and teacher, he is an accomplished painter whose work is showcased in the book, *Clarence Major and His Art: Portraits of an African-American Postmodernist.*

THOMAS MCGRATH was born on a North Dakota farm in 1916. During World War II he served in the Air Force, yet he was blacklisted for his political convictions during the McCarthy era. He worked as a documentary film scriptwriter, was founder and first editor of the literary magazine *Crazy Horse,* and received many literary awards. His books include *Selected Poems, Death Song,* and a massive booklength poem—and literary landmark—*Letter to an Imaginary Friend.* McGrath died in 1990, but has remained a constant deity in the cosmology of Copper Canyon Press.

W. S. MERWIN has been awarded most of the major prizes in American poetry, including the Pulitzer Prize, the Bollingen Prize, and the Tanning Prize for mastery in the art of poetry. He and his wife live on Maui, where he tends to his writing and to his garden of rare and endangered palm trees.

JANE MILLER currently lives in Tucson, where she is on the faculty of the Creative Writing Program at the University of Arizona. She has published seven volumes of poetry, including *Memory at These Speeds: New & Selected Poems* and *August Zero.* Her forthcoming book is *Palace of Pearls.*

PABLO NERUDA was born Neftali Ricardo Reyes Basoalto in Parral, Chile, in 1904. During his lifetime, he served as consul in Burma (now Myanmar) and held diplomatic posts in various East Asian and European countries. In 1945, a few years after he joined the Communist Party, Neruda was elected to the Chilean Senate. Shortly thereafter, when Chile's political climate took a sudden turn to the right, Neruda fled to Mexico and lived as an exile for several years. He later established a permanent home at Isla Negra. In 1970 he was appointed as Chile's ambassador to France, and in 1971 he was awarded the Nobel Prize in Literature. Pablo Neruda died in 1973. Seven volumes of his late and posthumous work have been published by Copper Canyon Press. The poems in this anthology were translated William O'Daly.

GREGORY ORR is the author of eight collections of poetry, including two books from Copper Canyon Press: *Orpheus & Eurydice: A Lyric Sequence* and *The Caged Owl: New and Selected Poems.* His fourth book of criticism, *Poetry as Survival,* was published by the University of Georgia Press in their "Life of Poetry" series, and his childhood memoir, *The Blessing,* appeared from Council Oak Books. He has taught at the University of Virginia since 1975, where he is a professor of English and poetry editor for the *Virginia Quarterly Review.*

CESARE PAVESE was born in the countryside outside Turin, Italy in 1908. At age 22 he earned a Ph.D. with a thesis on Walt Whitman, and in the 1930s became one of Italy's leading translators of American literature; his version of *Moby Dick* is still the standard. In 1935 he was jailed on the vague charge of "anti-Fascist activities," was sentenced to three years of detention, and was exiled to Brancaleone, Calabro. It was during this time he finished his first book, a collection of poems entitled *Lavorare stanca* (*Hard Labor*), the book he considered his masterpiece. He served ten months of his sentence, then returned to Turin and continued translating. In 1941 he published his first novel and ushered in a decade of ceaseless literary activity—by 1950 he had written nine novels and numerous novellas, short stories, poems, and critical essays. In May of 1950, at the peak of his career, he was awarded Italy's most coveted literary honor, the Premio Strega; in August he committed suicide, leaving these last words in his diary: "No words. An act. I won't write any more." His collection *Disaffections: Complete Poems, 1930–1950,* was translated by Geoffrey Brock.

ANTONIO PORCHIA was born in Italy in 1886 and died in Buenos Aires in 1968. In his introduction to his translations of Porchia's *Voices,* W.S. Merwin writes: "Little is publicly known beyond a few facts so bare that they would fit on any tombstone." After his father died, Porchia emigrated to Argentina with his mother and seven siblings. As the eldest child, he started working at the age of 14, first as a basketweaver. He later bought a print shop with his brother and worked there for years, never married, bought a house, and became the parental figure for his orphaned nieces and nephews. His first, small edition of *Voces* (*Voices*) was published in 1943, and then expanded and was republished in 1947. He caught the attention of a noted French critic who assumed him to be a scholar of Kafka and Buddhism, rather than a self-educated, humble man who loved to tend his garden.

MIKLÓS RADNÓTI, a Hungarian poet and translator, is considered one of his country's most important twentieth-century poets. Radnóti was killed in World War II during a forced march toward Germany. He was 35 years old. After the war Radnóti's last poems, written in a notebook during the march, were recovered from the mass grave in which he was buried. One of these final poems includes the lines: "Without commas, one line touching the other / I write poems the way I live, in darkness." Some of his poems appear in Stephen Berg's *The Steel Cricket: Versions 1958–1997.*

KENNETH REXROTH was born in 1905 in South Bend, Indiana. He was the author of nearly sixty books, including translations from Chinese, Japanese, Italian, and Swedish, and his *Classics* and *Classics Revisited,* among several volumes of essays. He was also one of the most original and universal literary scholars of the century. *The Complete Poems of Kenneth Rexroth* was published by Copper Canyon Press in 2002.

ALBERTO RÍOS teaches at Arizona State University and is the author of eight books of poetry, three collections of short stories, and a memoir about growing up on the Mexican border. He is the recipient of numerous awards and his poetry is included in over 175 national and international literary anthologies. His work is regularly taught and translated, and has been adapted to dance and to both classical and popular music. His book, *The Smallest Muscle in the Human Body,* was a finalist for the 2002 National Book Award in Poetry.

PRIMUS ST. JOHN was raised in New York City and has worked as a laborer, gambler, and civil servant. For the past twenty-eight years he has taught at Portland State University in Oregon. His most recent book of poetry is *Communion: Poems 1976–1998.*

DENNIS SCHMITZ is the author of six books of poetry, including *The Truth Squad* and *About Night: Selected and New Poems.* He has received numerous awards for his work, including the Shelley Memorial Award, two Pushcart Prizes, and fellowships from the Guggenheim Foundation and the National

Endowment for the Arts. He taught for over thirty years at California State University at Sacramento, and served as a poet laureate of Sacramento.

REBECCA SEIFERLE has published three books of poetry, including *Bitters* and a translation of Cesar Vallejo's *Trilce.* Her translation of Vallejo's *The Black Heralds/Los Heraldos Negros* is forthcoming in 2003. She is the publisher/ editor of the online poetry magazine, *The Drunken Boat,* and holds degrees from the University of the State of New York and Warren Wilson College. She lives and teaches in New Mexico.

ANN STANFORD was, throughout her career, a Californian poet. Born there in 1916, she attended Stanford University, earned her Ph.D. from UCLA, and taught at California State University, Northridge. She authored eight volumes of poetry and two verse plays, translated the classic Sanskrit text, *The Bhagavad Gita,* and edited *The Women Poets in English,* an anthology that gathered, for the first time, hundreds of years of poetry by women. She died in 1987.

RUTH STONE was born in Virginia in 1915. She is author of eight books of poems and was the recipient of the National Book Critics Circle Award. Her most recent book, *In the Next Galaxy,* won the 2002 National Book Award in Poetry. In 1959, after her husband died, she was forced to raise three daughters alone. For decades she traveled the United States, teaching creative writing at many universities, and finally settling at SUNY Binghamton. All the while she kept writing poetry. She lives in Vermont.

JOSEPH STROUD has been writing for more than thirty years, producing three tightly composed volumes of astonishing poetry, including *Below Cold Mountain, In the Sleep of Rivers,* and *Signatures.* He divides his time between Santa Cruz, California, and a small cabin on Shay Creek, on the eastern slope of the Sierra Nevada. A fourth book, *Country of Light,* is forthcoming in 2004.

ANNA SWIR (SWIRSZCZYNSKA) was born in Warsaw in 1909, the daughter of an impoverished painter. During World War II she was part of the Polish Resistance and wrote for underground publications. She died of cancer in 1984. Her poems were translated by Czeslaw Milosz and Leonard Nathan.

ARTHUR SZE is a second-generation Chinese American who was born in New York City in 1950. He graduated Phi Beta Kappa from the University of California at Berkeley and is the author of seven books of poetry and a book of translations. A professor of creative writing at the Institute of American Indian Arts, he lives in Pojoaque, New Mexico, with the poet Carol Moldaw and their daughter, Sarah.

TU FU (712–770), the "Poetry Sage" was born to a family that had once been part of nobility, but whose fortunes had declined. After failing his civil service examinations several times, he spent years wandering, living in poverty. He was a model of Confucian conduct and a poet whose inspiration came in large part from the suffering he observed during his travels, much of it the product of ruthless inscription and unfair taxation. His poetry went largely unacknowledged by all but his friend Li Po, and a few others, during his lifetime. Only 1,554 of his 10,000 poems survive. His poem appears in Arthur Sze's anthology of translations from the Chinese, *The Silk Dragon*.

REETIKA VAZIRANI's first book, *White Elephants,* was selected for the Barnard New Women Poets Prize. She was born in India, and her poems explore the ramifications of immigration and colonialism, particularly in her latest book, *World Hotel.* The recipient of a Discover award from *The Nation,* Vazirani serves as an advisory editor for *Callaloo.*

EMILY WARN, a former Stegner Fellow at Stanford University, holds degrees from Kalamazoo College and the University of Washington. She lives in Seattle and is the author of two books of poetry.

ELEANOR WILNER is the author of five books of poetry, including *Reversing the Spell: New & Selected Poems.* She holds a Ph.D. from Johns Hopkins University and serves as a contributing editor to *Calyx.* Her awards include a MacArthur Fellowship, the Juniper Prize, and a Pushcart Prize. Her forthcoming book is entitled *In the Meantime.*

C.D. WRIGHT has published nine collections of poetry, including the book-length poem, *Deepstep Come Shining,* and *Steal Away: Selected & New Poems.* In 1994 she was named State Poet of Rhode Island, a five-year post. On a fellowship for writers from the Lila Wallace-Reader's Digest Fund, she curated "a walk-in book of Arkansas," an exhibition which exploded and enlarged upon the idea of experiencing a book. Wright has also published a collaborative work with photographer Deborah Luster, entitled *One Big Self: Prisoners of Louisiana.* The project won the Lange-Taylor Prize from the Center for Documentary Studies at Duke University. Wright teaches at Brown University and edits Lost Roads Publishers with poet Forrest Gander. They live with their son, Brecht, near Providence, Rhode Island.

YANG CHU-YUAN (fl. 800) was a native of Shansi and at one time served as vice-governor of the southern half of the same province, and also as director of studies at the imperial university. According to Red Pine, the translator of *Poems of the Masters* (from which his poem is drawn), "The Chinese love to go looking for the first signs of spring, which usually include the blossoms of such fruit trees as the plum and the apricot. The Royal Woods (Shanlin) were a huge tract of pear and chestnut trees planted adjacent to the palace in Ch'ang-an during the Ch'in dynasty. They were later expanded during the Han dynasty well beyond the western suburbs. The Pa River, at the eastern edge of Ch'ang-an, was famous for its willow-lined banks. Yang suggests that the true connoisseur of spring is able to appreciate the willow's emerging golden catkins without feeling the need to wait for the more ostentatious show to come. In his commentary, Wang Hsiang says these images also refer to recognizing men of talent before they become known."

ABOUT THE EDITOR

MICHAEL WIEGERS is the editor of an anthology of poems about family, *The Poet's Child*, and co-editor, with Mónica de la Torre, of *Reversible Monuments: Contemporary Mexican Poetry*, both published by Copper Canyon Press.

The Chinese character for poetry is made up of two parts: "word" and "temple." It also serves as pressmark for Copper Canyon Press.

Founded in 1972, Copper Canyon Press remains dedicated to publishing poetry exclusively, from Nobel laureates to new and emerging authors. The Press thrives with the generous patronage of readers, writers, booksellers, librarians, teachers, students, and funders—everyone who shares the conviction that poetry invigorates the language and sharpens our appreciation of the world.

PUBLISHER'S CIRCLE
The Allen Foundation for the Arts
Lannan Foundation
National Endowment for the Arts

EDITOR'S CIRCLE
Thatcher Bailey
The Breneman Jaech Foundation
Cynthia Hartwig and Tom Booster
Target Stores
Emily Warn and Daj Oberg
Washington State Arts Commission

For information and catalogs:
COPPER CANYON PRESS
Post Office Box 271
Port Townsend, Washington 98368
360-385-4925
www.coppercanyonpress.org

This book was designed and typeset by Phil Kovacevich using QuarkXpress 4.1 on a Macintosh G4. The poems are set in Garamond, one of many typefaces based on the designs of the sixteenth-century printer, publisher, and type designer Claude Garamond. The Garamond typeface and its variations have been a standard among book designers and printers for four centuries. The poem titles are set in Requiem Display, a typeface derived from a set of inscriptional capitals appearing in Ludovico degli Arrighi's 1523 writing manual, *Il modo de temperare le penne.* This book was printed by Malloy Inc., Ann Arbor, Michigan.